Elemental Play and Outdoor Learning

Providing a fresh approach to examining development in the early years, this book draws together well-established ideas and theories based on outdoor play experiences and connects them to spiritual development in children.

Elemental Play and Outdoor Learning considers socio-cultural perspectives, guided participation and mediated learning alongside playfulness as it looks at young children's developing interest in the people around them, the environment they experience and the ideas and objects that involve them. Including rich encounters with young children and adults, chapters cover:

- elemental play as an approach to observe and support children's holistic development;
- the role of people in developing effective exploratory and social skills;
- using the concept of elemental play to consider the spiritual system as an aspect of child development;
- imaginative play with raw, natural materials and how prepared environments can encourage children's natural exploration;
- an exploration of well-established constructs of play and how elemental play can be integrated or re-conceptualised with the other theories.

Exploring current thinking about natural experiences, interest in forest school activity and fresh insight into dynamic ecological concepts, this book will be essential reading for practitioners and students on undergraduate and postgraduate early years and childhood studies courses.

Annie Woods is a former Senior Lecturer in Early Years at Nottingham Trent University, UK.

Elemental Play and Outdoor Learning

Young children's playful connections with people, places and things

Annie Woods

LONDON AND NEW YORK

First published 2017
by Routledge
2 Park Square, Milton Park, Abingdon, Oxon OX14 4RN

and by Routledge
711 Third Avenue, New York, NY 10017

Routledge is an imprint of the Taylor & Francis Group, an informa business

© 2017 Annie Woods

The right of Annie Woods to be identified as author of this work has been asserted by her in accordance with sections 77 and 78 of the Copyright, Designs and Patents Act 1988.

All rights reserved. No part of this book may be reprinted or reproduced or utilised in any form or by any electronic, mechanical, or other means, now known or hereafter invented, including photocopying and recording, or in any information storage or retrieval system, without permission in writing from the publishers.

Trademark notice: Product or corporate names may be trademarks or registered trademarks, and are used only for identification and explanation without intent to infringe.

British Library Cataloguing in Publication Data
A catalogue record for this book is available from the British Library

Library of Congress Cataloging-in-Publication Data
Names: Woods, Annie, author.
Title: Elemental play and outdoor learning : young children's playful connections with people, places and things / Annie Woods.
Description: New York, NY : Routledge, 2016. | Includes bibliographical references.
Identifiers: LCCN 2016022512| ISBN 9781138960701 (hardback) | ISBN 9781138960718 (pbk.) | ISBN 9781315660233 (ebook)
Subjects: LCSH: Outdoor education. | Play. | Early childhood education.
Classification: LCC LB1047 .W66 2016 | DDC 371.3/84—dc23
LC record available at https://lccn.loc.gov/2016022512

ISBN: 978-1-138-96070-1 (hbk)
ISBN: 978-1-138-96071-8 (pbk)
ISBN: 978-1-315-66023-3 (ebk)

Typeset in Bembo and Helvetica Neue
by Florence Production Ltd, Stoodleigh, Devon, UK

Contents

Foreword by Debbie Ryder vii
Acknowledgements viii

1 Elemental play: more than sand and water   1

2 Playing with people   15

3 Exploring the outdoor world with others   31

4 Awe and wonder   48

5 Being in one's element   62

6 The magic chocolate pit   78

7 Playing with things: children's ideas and projects   93

8 Playing naturally: outdoors and inside   107

9 Natural play connections   133

Index   155

Foreword

Annie Woods and I met on a bus at a Reggio Emilia tour and from there we have never looked back. What we were not to know was that not only would this be the beginning of a friendship that would sustain geographical challenges, but also from our collegial relationship a new play perspective would be conceived. As Annie discusses in the first chapter, it was on a visit to New Zealand in 2003 on the beautiful water's edge of Lake Wanaka that elemental play was 'born'. Like any newborn it was promptly named; also like all new babies, we had no idea what it was going to look like when it 'grew up'. Because we did not want to unduly influence its growth, we left elemental play to develop and develop. At times we would discuss the growing child and on one occasion we decided to tell others about it and we both wrote papers and presented on this 'growing' concept. We talked about our 'developing child' whenever we met up, in each other's respective countries, but only briefly; we just wanted to remind each other of its existence.

Each of us pondered about elemental play over the years, but it wasn't until thirteen years later that Annie decided it was time to take a good hard look at the development of elemental play. I am very grateful to Annie for her ability to, after all these years, not only capture the essence of those early conversations, but also legitimise elemental play alongside other literature.

Annie, courageously but tentatively, has taken on the task of positioning the existence of elemental play alongside key theoretical perspectives, while at the same time making this a text that is suitable for educators as a reflective tool. Children's learning stories (collected over the years) come to life on the pages as Annie weaves the child's learning with teachers' reflections and theory. The 'provocations' Annie adds at the end of each chapter remind us of the purpose of theorising, that is, to link to practice and reflection.

As Annie unravels the 'growth' of elemental play in this book, she talks of it as an instinctive, human and cultural disposition that links to young children's innate and spiritual relationships with people, places and things. Within elemental play, childhood is positioned as a playful, child-centred, socially constructed, active, creative, observational, imaginary and instinctive experience.

Debbie Ryder, Te Rito Maioba Early Childhood, New Zealand

Acknowledgements

The concept of elemental play was conceived, discussed and nurtured over a period of time and I would like to thank and acknowledge Debbie Ryder not only for the enduring relationship we enjoy but also for her critical yet affirming review of our ideas which have been presented in this book. I would also like to thank Justin Mills who, as a student, listened, argued and considered his own thoughts about the practice and approach he put into place in early years settings and within his own family. More thanks go to Hannah, leader of Little Muddy Boots, for the welcome received in the garden and for helping to give out and collect questionnaires from parents.

I am deeply grateful to my husband, Lemming, for his encouragement and insistence that I get these ideas down on paper. Finally, to Rosie Florence, our granddaughter, for arriving at just the right time, in more ways than one, to begin to enjoy the people, places and things that will envelop her childhood.

CHAPTER 1

Elemental play: more than sand and water

Whether exploring in the woods, on the beach or in the garden or jumping around in puddles, very young children's engagement, enjoyment and high level of involvement with the available loose materials which change with the weather and the season is a constant delight to me. Perhaps more interesting are the *actions* with, on and in the materials that children show. Like you, I have watched hundreds of children play and have played myself as a child; what I did in the sand, I saw my own children and other children do; what I did with water is also repeated through the generations. Sand, mud, sticks, stones, cones, shells, petals, leaves and logs, we reach out, we pick up, we mix, we transport, we taste, we pile up, we dig down, we scrape and gauge, we build up and knock down, we cover up and collect, we throw, we make shelter and we make marks. We run, climb, lie down, jump, laugh in and shelter from the rain, huddle round bright fires and chase the wind; we look for and find small creatures and evidence of larger creatures. Like first explorers or hunter-gatherers, a woodland, a park, a hill, a river, a forest, a garden or a meadow is discovered by children anew, even though 'it was always there'.

This chapter introduces and explores the concept of elemental play. It is more than playing with sand and water; rather, it suggests a lens through which to observe and support children's holistic development. Barrows (1995: 103) has suggested that

> a new theory of child development must be evolved. Such a theory must take into consideration that the infant is born into not only a social but an ecological context. It must acknowledge that from the earliest moments of life, the infant has an awareness not only of human touch, but of the touch of the breeze on her skin, variations of light and colour, temperature, texture and sound.

Vasta (1992: 277) reassures that 'No one approach to understanding child development is going to sweep the board. Any new approach is to be judged by the extent to which they can be integrated with previous ones.'

Children's projects and the emergence of an idea

Debbie Ryder and I began a conversation in 2003 beside Lake Wanaka, New Zealand, that explored the interconnectedness between people, places and things in relation to natural surroundings, first by discussing the Te Whāriki curriculum (Ministry of Education, 1996) and the idea of *projettizone* (projects) documented in Reggio Emilia. Following a visit made in 2001 to Reggio where we had met, Debbie had embarked on a series of projects provoked by the children in her centre and the local community environment and by staff who were actively making observations of children and their ideas.

Debbie and I began to consider the process of developing interests (Figure 1.1).

We considered the word 'project' to mean a quest, an inquiry, or an exploration. What next emerged in our conversation was the overwhelming interest and exploratory drive we had observed in young children in connection with natural materials and the elements of life. These interests and explorations necessarily involved the people concerned with the child and the environments they encountered during their explorations. Debbie discussed her observations of children being more at ease with certain people, with familiar objects or in safe places. I was not convinced that very young children could *design* projects if projects are taken to mean forward planning (pro) and, subsequently, the decision to work with an ob(ject) or series of objects. Certainly we had both seen children with obvious schemas, transporting objects from one place to another, building and collecting things in lines, and being interested in the trajectory of objects but the question of whether children who are pre-verbal, often only just emerging as independently mobile, can be capable of projecting ideas continues to form an ongoing dialogue. Our model of elemental play began to develop (Figure 1.2).

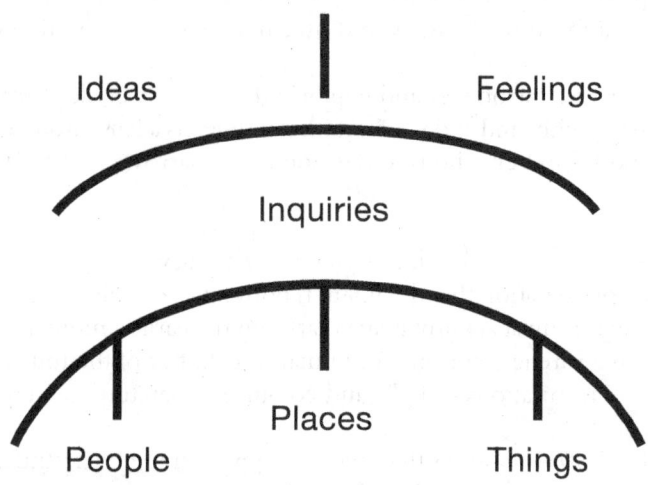

FIGURE 1.1 Developmental umbrella

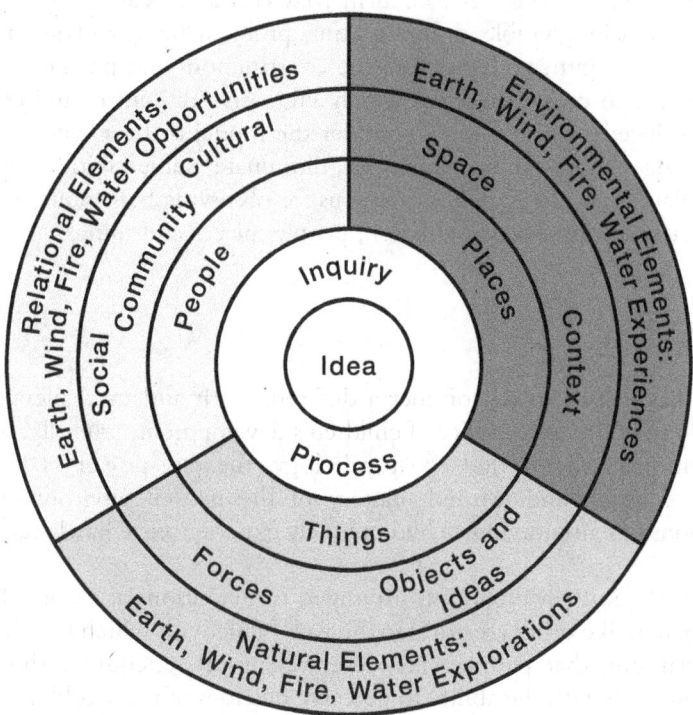

FIGURE 1.2 Elemental play

It is no coincidence that there is synergy with the New Zealand early years curriculum:

> Children learn through responsive and reciprocal relationships with people, places and things. The learning environment will assist children in their quest for making sense of and finding out about their world if there are active and interactive learning opportunities for children to have an effect and to change the environment.
>
> (Ministry of Education, 1996: 19)

> Children develop the ability to enquire, research, explore, generate, and modify their own working theories about the natural, social, physical, and material worlds; about Planet Earth and beyond; a relationship with the natural environment and a knowledge of their own place in the environment including myths and legends and oral, non-fictional forms.
>
> (Ibid.: 90)

This diagrammatic notion of elemental play resonates with many other ideas, theories and approaches which will be explored in detail throughout this book.

Dahlberg et al. (1999: 34, cited in Maynard and Waters, 2014: 2) suggest that 'through making visible, deconstructing, problematizing and questioning dominant discourses, regimes of truth and the constructions and practices they produce, it is possible to create spaces in which alternative discourses and constructions can be produced'. Debbie and I consider the model to be a synergy of ideas, a tool 'weaving theory and practice to illuminate subjectivities' (Smith, cited in MacNaughton, 2005: 57); it is a locus for observing behaviour and also exploring the relationship between children, people, places and things.

Ecology

This has helped us to consider a different truth and to challenge the dominant ideology of the universality of children's development; crucially, it appears to link evolutionary theory and eco-psychology, the raw power of the elements and socio-cultural, and learned mastery of the natural environment through the relationships an individual child uniquely experiences. Chawla (2006: 63) has said:

> Ecological psychology is grounded in evolutionary theory. It views human beings like other creatures in the web of life with which they have co-evolved, claiming that people, like other organisms, encounter the physical world directly, with the ability to perceive qualities of the world that are really there rather than merely mental constructions about the world. It assumes that human beings are dependent on intrinsic qualities of the physical world, its resources and limits, and they can discover what these resources and limits are through direct perception in order to adjust their behaviour in adaptive ways.

The Te Whāriki (Ministry of Education, 1996) curriculum, is grounded in Maori traditions and culture:

> For the Maori, the creation was central to his relationship to other kin and to the world around him: the birds, insects, plants, fish and natural phenomena like the moon, rain, mist and wind. This close and intimate relationship with all things was expressed in what we call *whakapapa* (geneology). It is about love and respect for our culture, our fellow man and our environment.
> (*Taonga Maori*, 1989: 18–21)

Cahalan (1995: 217) suggests that 'Ecological groundedness is a dynamic state of the person that includes the sense of confidence, pleasure, and wonder resulting from progressively deepening contact with the world and domesticated natural community of the person's neighbourhood and larger land region'. This echoes

> Dewey's (1915) recognition of the centrality and interconnectedness of experiences in learning. Experience has its geographical aspect, its artistic and its literary, its scientific and its historical sides. All studies arise from aspects of

one earth and the one life lived upon it . . . we live in a world where all sides are bound together. All studies grow out of relations in the one great common world.

(Wattchow and Brown, 2011: 195)

Mills wrote in 2006:

> central to the philosophy of elemental play is the idea that the child is protagonist in their learning but also that children seem to have a preference for areas rich in natural elements. Kahn and Kellert (2002) believe that these early relationships with nature are sources of well-being and funds of strength in later life. One of the reasons for this intuitive actions towards natural elements could be the idea of 'archaic consciousness'.
>
> 'Archaic experience is elemental in an immediate physical sense. It is a way of being baptized into the world by immersion, such as children in play who literally live close to the ground and up against the full sensory quality of things – making hiding places under tables and bushes, climbing trees, rolling down hills, squatting in the mud and water, and peering under rocks, surrounded by smell, textures and details that the adult height and habits will later remove from them' (Kahn and Kellert, 2002: 209).
>
> This profound notion suggests that very young children are drawn to the elements because they are experiencing a sense of identity and re-cognition of the elements which it is believed human life originated. They further argue (ibid.: 215) that this archaic or magic consciousness 'cannot be spied by observation, and even less can we question children about them'.
>
> Perhaps young children's fascination with the elements is somehow connected to our evolution as a species and our close relationship with environment as a means of survival.

Rupp (2005: 344) suggests:

> What makes us all the intelligent, insightful and delightful people we hope we are is a dauntingly complex mix of genetic, physiological, psychological, evolutionary, and environmental factors, melded in some unspecified fashion to make each of us unique. For all our differences, humans share many behavioural, emotional, and cognitive traits which predict, more or less, how we're likely to learn, adapt to changing environments, and interact in social situations.

Spiritual development

The concept of elemental play may provide us with a means to recognise children's holistic development, which includes a spiritual dimension hitherto not fully considered but explored further in Chapter 4. It also considers shared meanings experienced between a child and others in their biophilic relationship with the natural environment and constancy of the elements. It will be argued throughout this book that elemental play is an instinctive, human and cultural disposition and observed in children as an overwhelming and intensive drive to be re-connected the earth, water, wind and fire: a cultural, spiritual and genetic fingerprint.

The elemental play model is rhizomatic, allowing for a layering of ideas and differential development in children, nurtured by the people, places and things encountered and 'laid down' by genetic inheritance. A plant rhizome grows and develops from a bulb which adds bulbs under the ground (and unseen) to produce more shoots. Deleuze and Guattari (1987: 21, cited in MacNaughton, 2005: 119) suggest that 'The rhizome operates by variation, expansion, conquest, capture, offshoots', thus each new bulb will grow, but dependent on the genetic disposition of the original bulb and the environmental conditions which it meets that nurture further growth. We can say, then, that elemental play is a form of rhizomatic epigenesis:

> Epigenesis is the emergence of new structures and functions during the course of development' (Gottlieb, 1991a: 7). It reflects a bidirectional relationship among all levels of biological and experiential factors, such that genetic activity both influences and is influenced by structural maturation, which is bi-directionally related to function and activity.
>
> (Bjorkland and Pellegrini, 2002: 33)

In other words, the dynamic interplay of nature and nurture. Using rhizoanalysis to look at child development allows us to consider all the many connections between theories and our own observational interpretations. The contextual environment of the development is crucial to any post-structural interpretation of behaviour. Bjorkland and Pellegrini (2002: 43) further propose that

> human nature is not something that is simply 'innate', 'instinctive' or 'within the organism'; rather, human nature develops. Human beings (and all animals) are born with genetically influenced dispositions that have been shaped by millions of years of natural selection. These dispositions interact with all levels of the environment producing species-typical patterns of development.
>
> Evolutionary developmental psychology assumes that not only are the behaviours and cognitions that characterise adults the product of natural selection, but so are characteristics of children's behaviours and minds. Evolved psychological mechanisms interact with the local environment to produce a particular pattern of behaviour. It is the similarity of the species' environment, as well as the similarities of a species' genome, that is responsible for the universal physical, behavioural, and psychological features that humans share. To the extent that individuals grow up in environments similar to those of their ancestors, development should follow a species-typical pattern.

Theoretical connections

To explore, exploit and enjoy the environment; these are observable dispositions we see in our very youngest children. Elemental play embraces the ideas of Dewey, Piaget, Vygotsky, Gardner, Bruner, Athey, Bowlby and Bronfenbrenner. It is a dynamic, ecological model of early development and behaviour. It suggests that a child is drawn to and demonstrates well-being when playing in a natural context that is culturally and ecologically *familiar*. It also suggests that very young children's interests can be quite deeply spiritual as they re-connect with the earth's elements. We consistently see children playing and being excited by natural materials, reflecting the functional exploration of hunter-gatherer type behaviour: digging a pit, damming a stream, bridging a gap, making a shelter, building a fire and collecting sticks and stones for tools. We see young children drawn to water as they experience flow, cause and effect. Water is an element with pre-natal memories and early tactile and affective satisfaction. Children love and become excited by wind and air flow – soon becoming tired as the flow/current is greater than the individual. Children become 'windy' and as 'high as kites' after blowy play and love the force of air upon things. Children are drawn – when permitted – to light and heat, whether fire, lights, sparks, or the contrast of light and dark. Reggio Emilia projects often reflect this observed interest. These are all natural forces or elements. As adults, we feel an emotional resonance to movement, light and space in the landscape and this will be explored in Chapter 3.

Children appear to be content for longer when handling natural materials. This is more extensive than calling it heuristic or exploratory play. It seems to be more fundamental (elemental) than that. It is more than play with natural objects; it is also about the environmental and spiritual use and respect of elements. When we observe and interpret pre-verbal communication and thinking, albeit with our own subjectivities and 'net' (Eisner, 1985, cited in Whitehead, 1992: 93), we might say that children are demonstrating a biocultural and innate interest in reading, interpreting, and making meaning and connections between elements in order to survive, mature, gain mastery of and belong. If children are not given opportunities to explore their own ideas through action with elemental forces, inquiries may become limited and mastery/confidence remain under-developed. These connections develop into what Piaget would claim to be processes of assimilation and adaption, establishing equilibrium and, at times, experience of disequilibrium when a new cause or effect destabilises what has already been learned. Elemental play, therefore, may be said to lift mental and environmental awareness: ele[mental].

People, places and things

Put simply, the elemental play model presents what Debbie and I believe is a hypothesis for child development: a child observed as having an idea, or an exploratory drive or desire. The child then chooses or gravitates towards a relationship or attachment with a person, a place or a thing depending on the environmental context, and the thing may be an object or an idea. The adults who live, play and work alongside the child and who work in an environment affording experiential learning are more likely to satisfy the child's quest. The quest, and feeling of well-being experienced particularly with the elements, appears to have an emotional and spiritual resonance with the child. Carson (1998: 56 in Kahn and Kellert, 2002: 126) recalls:

> For the child . . . it is not half so important to *know* as to *feel*. If facts are the seeds that later produce knowledge and wisdom, then the emotions and the impressions of the senses are the fertile soil in which the seeds must grow. The years of early childhood are the time to prepare the soil. Once the emotions have been aroused – a sense of the beautiful, the excitement of the new and the unknown, a feeling of sympathy, pity, admiration or love – then we wish for knowledge about the object of our emotional response. Once found, it has lasting meaning. It is more important to pave the way for the child to want to know than to put him on a diet of facts he is not ready to assimilate.

Our role as practitioners can be represented as in Figure 1.3.

The child has an idea, follows an enquiry in a people or places or things direction, experiencing and engaging with natural, social, environmental or emotional elements in a continuous coil of action; the adult then provokes the

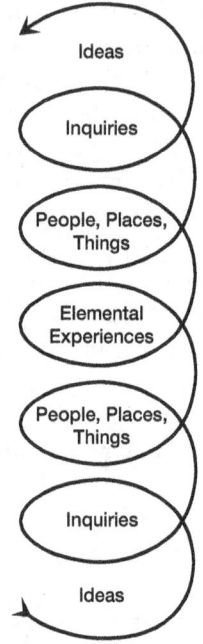
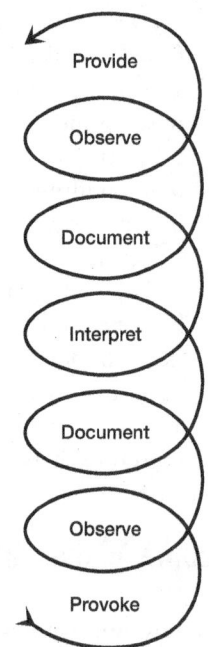

FIGURE 1.3 Elemental coil

child by presenting an opportunistic but planned environment, observes the child's enquiries, documents the action and interprets the activity and further provokes/extends/supports the child in their continued activity. Mills (2006), past student, now experienced practitioner and teacher, sent me the following encounter.

ENCOUNTER: William, Bonnie and Louie

Louie is very familiar with his uncle William. They spent Louie's first nine months together in the same house and have a loving relationship. Louie and Bonnie met fleetingly last year at Mudeford and this year they have spent several days playing together. They are in the midst of building a warm and affectionate relationship.

For some reason throwing has featured significantly in our family history. It is almost customary for my brother and I to visit the water's edge for a spot of stone throwing. We spend hours looking for the perfect skimmer, chat and catch up. Upon reflection, these moments have a ceremonial quality. They happen at certain times and very often in a similar place – the harbour shoreline. They seem to occur when we have just met, perhaps not having seen one another for a period of months. They are moments when we are reconnecting with each other and at Mudeford.

Today was no different from many other years. My brother and I met up and somehow ended up at the water's edge – stones in hands. This *was* different, however. A new generation to Mudeford, Louie and Bonnie, had decided to join us. The dynamics were completely different. I intuitively felt that this was an important moment. Camera loaded, I stepped back from the proceedings and watched.

William hurled stones deep into the belly of the harbour, almost oblivious to Louie and Bonnie. There is a deep satisfaction and a sense of dynamic release in the act of throwing, particularly into water. William was absorbed in a world of flight, collision and trajectory. I wonder what Louie and Bonnie think as they watch him?

William searches the carpet of seaweed diligently, burrows briefly and emerges with something that he examines in depth. The stone is rolled around in his hands as he stands upright and scans the harbour. His knees are bent as he tilts backwards in the style of a pole-vaulter. Suddenly he runs full pelt towards the water in a half-crouched crab-like manoeuvre. Bonnie and Louie are rooted as William launches the pebble skyward. In the moment of flight, stillness precedes a dramatic opening of the water. A volcanic-like eruption signifies that pebble and water have collided. Rings of small waves ripple and conceal the stone's identity. The water behaves like nothing ever happened. Bonnie and Louie stand together and watch this whole brief but engaging moment.

A flurry of activity begins. Bonnie stands furthest back from the shoreline and watches William and Louie. Louie busily searches for large stones to throw into the water and occasionally watches William throwing and skimming. Bonnie fiddles with her t-shirt and carefully inches closer to William and Louie. The group are now close together, near the shoreline. A nearby swan stands proudly in the shallows as it preens and shakes its tail feathers. From the perspective of a very young child this could be a threatening experience, yet they continue with their activity of stone throwing.

Louie points to a white swan feather bobbing in the shallow water and ventures in to collect it. Up till now, the group have selected stones that all sink when they come into contact with water. The feather is striking in appearance and the way it floats on water; is it the way the feather dances on the water that attracts Louie? Does he wonder whether it belongs to the swan? Louie brings William into his exploration by handing the feather to him. The feather is reunited with the water and survives a spell of target practice before it is gently taken away by incoming tide.

Louie and Bonnie play near the water's edge. Bonnie is growing in curiosity and moves ever closer to the water until her shoes touch the water's edge. She chuckles and points to the water as Louie squats and plays with the soft textures of seaweed, sand and froth. Up until now dogs, boats, aeroplanes, bikes and people pass by but fail to attract attention.

Louie notices a collie perched on top of the rocks, watching the harbour. Louie begins a vertical ascent up to the first three tiers of rock. He scans the rocks with hands, feet and eyes, looking for a potential route. Louie looks up and talks to the dog in a friendly tone, but the dog takes little notice. Louie's tone sounds like he is asking the dog a question. Might he be inviting the dog to join them or could he be wondering what the dog is looking at? Whatever Louie is thinking, he is trying to connect with the dog and he now, like the dog, faces out to the harbour. He appears to have another idea forming.

He sets himself the challenge of travelling horizontally: rock to rock. This varied terrain is ever changing, offering a multitude of perspectives, choices and experiences. On the rocks, Louie has to make decisions that require the ability to accurately judge distance and stability, there is no pause in his action. Standing on the lip of a large, flat rock, Louie holds onto a rock just ahead of him. A stepping stone lies between the large rocks. Louie is now standing on the stepping stone – on tiptoe. The awkward stepping stone (lying on a horizontal angle of forty-five degrees) poses a dilemma. He clings on to a rock with arms and hands, unsure whether to go back or carry on. He looks down and notices a small plateau at the top of the stepping stone. This enables a firm footing to carry him onto the rock ahead.

He has made it. These moments of intense concentration culminate in a broad smile as he stands upright. He chats to the uninterested dog and finds a potential route for getting to the third and final tier of rocks – a diagonal slope of rock. After several attempts, Louie decides to keep moving in a horizontal direction. This time, however, there is a crevice between the rocks. He crouches down and forms a bridge by stretching across the gap with his hands. Again, Louie faces the problem of not being able to go back and has committed himself to finding a way forwards. He calmly looks towards his feet and notices a stone conveniently bridging the gap. He places a foot on the stone and successfully moves across. Upright, he looks towards Bonnie and William and plans his descent. He considers and seems to reject the idea of stepping off the edge of the rock. It is too far to fall. Louie chuckles as he sits down and clambers stomach first off the rock.

On the ground, Louie finds a long branch that he takes to the shoreline. He places one end on the sand and lifts the branch to a vertical position. He moves the branch and watches the top of the branch move in the air. He must feel a real sense of control and empowerment at being able to manipulate such a long and large object.

In the background, I notice Bonnie trying to make a connection with William. Bonnie strides towards him with a feather held aloft. It is a gift that has the effect of gaining his attention and interest. Louie moves closer to William and Bonnie and lays his branch down as he takes off his shoes. He is on an area of soft sand – kind on the feet. Louie crouches on the shoreline, picks up his branch and places the hooked tip into the crystal clear water. He looks intently at the submerged tip, which, due to refraction, appears to have taken on a different form. With one hand, Louie drags the branch into the water. This is an opportunity to test many ideas. After a brief exploration in the water, he takes the branch back onto the sand and stands it in an upright position before returning to the water. The curvy shape of the branch means that in shallow water, some of it is above and some below the water. Louie lets go and watches it as it rocks to and fro in a jerky rhythm with the incoming tide. Louie watches. The tide moves the tip of the stick away from the shoreline and out towards the harbour. Louie follows. The end of the branch protrudes from the water. Louie crouches in the water. He pulls and pushes and watches attentively as this snake-like object slithers through the water. Bonnie watches and responds by finding and throwing sticks into the water. It's interesting to note that both Bonnie and Louie have moved on to exploring sticks simultaneously.

Bonnie and Louie are full of purpose and energy as they find and collect sticks and feathers. Both children now have their shoes off and appear totally absorbed in their environment. Louie finds a dead crab; legs and body fragments offer an engaging structure which Louie crushes. Bonnie then hunts for crabs herself. With a feather in hand, she investigates the shoreline. She scans the ground intensely, crouching, gently turning stones and looking under seaweed until she finds the remains of a crab. She finds the upper shell and stands up to take a good look at it. She holds the crab shell carefully with two hands, staring deeply at it whilst feeling the serrated perimeter of the crab's shell with her fingers.

Louie has now decided to take his nappy off. As the children have become more involved in their play, they have dressed in less and less clothing! Louie now has the opportunity to fully experience his surroundings.

He plays at the shoreline, investigating the soft textures of sand, froth and weed, and looking up to see a swan swimming past. Without hesitation, Louie walks towards the swan and babbles in an excited tone. The swan plunges its neck below the water line and emerges with a beak dripping with weed. Louie watches and ventures further in. The cold water rises as he comes to an abrupt halt. He turns to the shore with an outstretched hand and motions William to come in. He looks as though he wants to go further out but he is cautious. He has experienced swimming pools so has some concept of deeper water.

In his final moments at the water's edge, Louie explores with his body; lowering the bottom part of his body in the water, he smiles and this marks the end of this passage of play.

My response to Louie as a child and to Justin Mills as his father began further discussions about elemental play. Louie is determined to explore the *place* of the beach through his control, manipulation and relationship with his father. He connects to the feel of the place and the *things* he finds. He is very drawn to the *people* who support his elemental play. Many of his actions are imitative, although he initiates activity. His gaze appears to demonstrate a sense of wonder, important for well-being, and his place in time and spirit. When he takes his shoes off, the soft sand becomes a boundary; he dances as if in ritual. He appears *in his element*, taking a personal ownership of this stretch of beach. His elemental play is extended by adults' attuned mutuality. He wallows in the textures, smells and sights of the shore, getting to know what he can lift, taste, smell, control, throw, climb onto and feel. He assesses risks for himself. The elemental play concept thus illustrates:

- the power that people are willing to share with children's self-determination;
- the power of the elements and the socio-cultural learned mastery of the natural environment;
- the power and truth of children's unique ideas that are rarely vocalised but regularly observed.

What we also observe is generational behaviour; how Louie stands at the beach is how my son used to stand at the beach, and also countless children when confronting the all-powerful sea and with easy access to objects that can be controlled by children as they determine to achieve self-mastery and experience cause and effect. The physical stance is also physiologically similar in many two year olds. Isaacs, recalled by Rich et al. (2008, cited in Maynard and Waters, 2014: 32) may also see this observation and beach as:

- a rich treasure chest of an *environment*, with an abundance of interesting 'stuff' for children to handle;
- the availability of *'big ideas'* – investigating and making sense of the real world;
- an abundance of *time* for doing and thinking that is uninterrupted and not pre-structured.

The young children were accompanied by familiar people who were watching rather than participating. The beach was a familiar place as were some of the familiar things. Our exploration of elemental play can and has taken place in preschool, school gardens and rooms, kindergartens, home gardens, woodland and front rooms. Very young children seem to be drawn/feel comfortable with particular people, feel secure in distinct spaces or environments and, sometimes, attached to certain objects. On a walk around my house with five-month-old Rosie yesterday, we stopped at every picture on the wall, and she greeted it with open mouth and soft, almost 'hello' sound – 'ahh-oo'; this is part of our familiarising ritual when she is looked after outside her parents' house. She makes the same noise at a particular picture in a book – a grandmother with hair tied back, mouth open singing. Later in the day we had our first real walk in the garden, and for thirty minutes named and touched the shrubs and trees before sitting on a bench to listen to the birds. She was very still, even her legs, which are usually active and exploring. I expect that in future, repeated walks, we will begin to hear the 'aah-oo' noise as we revisit the catkins and buds. Her exploration is at the stage of needing support from a familiar adult, but given the opportunity of tactile, communicative, sensual relationships with people who are modelling a deep love of the outdoors and elemental experiences, it will be interesting to see how her unique ideas and inquiries progress.

Provocations

- Kahn and Kellert (2002) ask us to reflect on the extent to which direct and indirect experience of nature is a critical component in human physical, emotional, intellectual and moral development. Further, 'do young children form deep connections with the natural world, or is that idea actually a myth?' (2002: vii). What are your initial reactions to the idea of elemental play? What has it helped you remember or connect?
- Is elemental play a new concept or is it recognising something that was already there but not named? What are you bringing to mind on these thoughts?
- Is there a role for elemental play in the twenty-first-century urban child?
- Does elemental play represent a generational echo?

References

Barrows, A. (1995) The ecopsychology of child development. In T. Roszak, M.E. Gomes and A.D. Kanner (eds) *Ecopsychology: Restoring the Earth/Healing the Mind*. San Francisco: Sierra Club Books, pp. 101–10.

Bjorkland, D.F. and Pellegrini, A.D. (2002) *The Origins of Human Nature. Evolutionary Developmental Psychology*. Washington, DC: American Psychological Association.

Cahalan, W. (1995) Ecological groundedness in gestalt therapy. In T. Roszak, M.E. Gomes and A.D. Kanner (eds) *Ecopsychology: Restoring the Earth/Healing the Mind*. San Francisco: Sierra Club Books, pp. 216–23.

Chawla, L. (2006) Learning to love the world enough to protect it. www.ntnu.no/documents/10458/19133135/Chawla1.pdf (accessed 14 September 2015).

Kahn, Jr. P.H. and Kellert, S.R. (eds) (2002) *Children and Nature. Psychological, Sociocultural and Evolutionary Investigations*. Cambridge, MA: MIT Press.

MacNaughton, G. (2005) *Doing Foucault in Early Childhood Studies: Applying Poststructural Ideas*. Abingdon: Routledge.

Maynard, T. and Waters, J. (2014) *Exploring Outdoor Play in the Early Years*. Maidenhead: Oxford University Press.

Mills, J. (2006) Elemental play: exploring a notion of socio cultural adult/child play that links intuitive connections with nature with a holistic approach to development. Unpublished MA thesis, Sheffield University.

Ministry of Education (1996) *Te Whāriki*. Wellington, NZ: Learning Media.

Rupp, R. (2005) *Four Elements: Water, Air, Fire, Earth*. London: Profile Books.

Taonga Maori: A Spiritual Journey Expressed Through Maori Art (1989) National Museum Guide. Wellington, NZ: Te Papa Press.

Vasta, R. (ed.) (1992) *Six Theories of Child Development: Revised Formulations and Current Issues*. London: Jessica Kingsley.

Wattchow, B. and Brown, M. (2011) *A Pedagogy of Place. Outdoor Education for a Changing World*. Clayton, Vic., Australia: Monash University Publishing.

Whitehead, M. (1992) Assessment at key stage 1: core subjects and the developmental curriculum. In G.M. Blenkin and A.V. Kelly (eds) *Assessment in Early Childhood Education*. London: PCP, pp. 93–121.

CHAPTER

2

Playing with people

This chapter explores more deeply the crucial role of *people* in the developing relationships children encounter with the places and the things of the world. It is predicated on the following assumptions:

- Children construct understanding through an active, exploratory drive.
- Children assimilate experiences and connect new sensations and activities with earlier encounters and accommodate new information.
- Early encounters are mediated through social interactions.
- The role of adults is one of nurture, protection and the sharing of cultural values through reciprocal exchange.

Kahn and Kellert (2002: 9) confirm that

> Much has been written about emotions of attachment, belonging, and security in nonhuman and human primates. For example, most, but not all, available evidence suggests that a youngster's secure attachment to the primary care giver generally allows for the development of effective exploratory and social skills.

The elemental play idea emerged from discussion and dialogue in New Zealand and reflects the foundation of the Te Whāriki (Ministry of Education, 1996) curriculum which embeds a close bond between people, places and things and reflects a number of socio-cultural lenses through which this book is positioned. In creating the concept of elemental play, it is argued that children appear to have an exploratory desire to engage with the outdoor environment. This desire, it is argued, is both natural and nurtured through the emerging and extending relationships with the people who care for them. Elemental play is a socio-cultural and two-way transitional perspective on learning and development which interconnects infancy to adulthood and adults to children. The natural environment is argued to be the elemental essence of and for young children; it is within the child fully, but can and seems to weaken over time, particularly for those not afforded the opportunities for regular and extensive exploration outdoors with attuned and supportive adults who both teach and help children learn through increasingly challenging opportunities. The natural elements provide an environment for joint attention, sustained shared thinking and mutual cultural consciousness.

In this chapter, the following aspects will be discussed:

- Socio-cultural transitional perspective – a two-way lifelong learning process with infants learning to adapt to their cultural context; this involves the use of actual, social and linguistic tools with the support of knowledgeable others.
- Mediated learning – adults mediating the introduction and continuity of natural experiences for children and the scaffolding of experiences for children; Rogoff (1990) calls this 'guided participation'.
- Joint attention – and how this influences the interconnected relationship between infant and adult.
- Sustained shared thinking – and how this is an outcome from the reciprocal two-way relationship between child and adult.

The further aspect of playfulness – as natural playful learning where children encounter the world on their own terms – will be explored in greater detail in Chapters 8 and 9.

Natural exploration

The evidence of elemental play appears to be more obvious in very young children before more formal experiences compete with their playful interests and they become increasingly influenced by adverse cultural attitudes towards natural exploration, risky play and the everyday messiness of the very materials they are attracted to.

This encounter took place in Oliver's first visit to forest school. It is obvious out in the woods at our forest school sessions, where, with no prepared activities or outcomes, the three-year-old children are definitely at ease, or in their element with the trees, the cloud-studded sky, the rain, the mud and the tall plants, as if, like first explorers or hunters, they have a desire to master/overcome/survive and use the natural materials. My role as adult is to share or mediate their curious and creative delights.

ENCOUNTER: Oliver and the deep puddle

Oliver had taken some time to settle after his mum had left him to play in the woods with us. He was reluctant to put on waterproofs but watched the other children intently as they walked up and down the puddle. He began to tentatively put his boot into the edge of the squelch. He asked for the waterproof dungarees. He looked at me: 'Do you know where my feet go?' 'Come and play. Look out! Come in here, you can . . .

> Can you get me out of here? How much giant steps do I need to do...? 1, 2 I need to do 1, 2. 1 ... 2, 2, 2, 2, 2.' Oliver walks up and down the length of the ten foot muddy puddle, trailing through the watery mud. He goes down on his haunches. He kicks and splashes. I am very close by.
>
> To me: 'Watch out for the deeper bits. Oh, plough, you come in, go in here. Oh squished, let me go in it, let me have in. I just went straight, turn it.' He is much quicker now, almost running. Two other children join Oliver who is stamping up and down.
>
> To me: 'Can you tell me to watch out for the deep bit? You look at me while I go. Can you tell me again? Can I walk through it?' Oliver walks over to one of the other puddles, I stay where I am. He comes back, slips and is on all fours. He is not worried. He goes over to another adult to get a little cleaned up and returns, running up and down, stamping.
>
> To me: 'Let's go and play in that giant piece of water.'
>
> Oliver had been engaged for over an hour; my participation was engaged rather than guided but Oliver may have perceived my presence as an emotional guide for his tentative then growing confidence in the puddle play as he constantly invited me to participate.

Evolutionary connections

The idea of elemental play is suggestive of an evolutionary connection to that 'that was always there', which the human species constantly strive to understand, explore and overcome, like children learning to be in the world. Here, adults' joint attention is crucial in both remembering what it is like to be a child and being on hand to help where expert skills can be shared with children. It is crucial, therefore, for adults to afford opportunities to children to make of the world what they will and, by watching closely, and to observe very young children play in the same way as every generation of children has played. Adults do not play like children and elemental play suggests something deeper in this play activity – a collective and cultural memory of play and learning through the natural environment. In Chapter 4, a further element of spiritual memory is discussed.

> ### ENCOUNTER: Lara in the woods
>
> Lara places a tarpaulin in the clearing and lies down. Andrew lies next to her sucking his thumb. Angel joins them.
>
> Lara: 'Its absolutely beautiful. I love the sun dappling through the trees. I like the colours.'
>
> The two children look up, silently watching the gentle movement of the leaves above.
>
> Forest school leader Lara shares her thoughts with the children, marvelling at a natural and beautiful experience.

Hinde (in Vasta, 1992: 255) argues that

> Relationships, groups and certain aspects of the sociocultural structure form the most important part of the environment of individuals, but the physical environment also is important, itself affecting and affected by the behaviour of individuals. And all these levels of social complexity, the sociocultural structure and the environment, exist in time, and cannot be fully understood independently of their history. It means that an understanding of child development requires an appreciation not only of both the biological and the social forces determining its course, but also of the relations between them.

Rogoff (2003: 3) is similarly persuasive; based on many years of research and field study in South America. She says:

> human development is a cultural process. As a biological species, humans are defined in terms of our cultural participation. We are prepared by both our cultural and biological heritage to use language and other cultural tools and to learn from each other.

She further states 'Humans develop through their changing participation in the sociocultural activities of their communities, which also change' (p. 11). This 'changing participation' is the foundation of Bronfenbrenner's (1979) ecological systems theory and is the model upon which the concept of elemental play is based, that 'the acquisition of knowledge and understanding stems not only from exploration but also from mediated social practice (Bruner 1983; Rogoff, 1990) and communication', described as 'culturally organised activity' by Rogoff (1990), cited in May et al. (2006: 41).

Oyama (2002b: 29, in Bjorkland and Pellegrini, 2002: 35) considers the epigenetic (nature and nurture) foundation of Bronfenbrenner's theory of nested communities that evolve and widen as a child develops:

> What is transmitted between generations is not traits, or blueprints, or symbolic representations of traits, but developmental *means (or resources, or interactants)*. These means include genes, the cellular machinery necessary for their functioning, and the larger developmental context, which may include a maternal reproductive system, parental care, or other interaction with conspecifics, as well as relations with other aspects of the animate and inanimate worlds. This context, which is actually a system of partially nested contexts, changes with time, partly as a result of developmental processes themselves.

Child–environment–adult relations

It has always been useful to have a third person share interpretations and discuss the ideas that Debbie Ryder and I have had, and Mills (2006) responded:

Elemental play draws on an inter-related process of connectedness between child and environment and adult, with the environment being the inter-connecting factor. Memories of play in the natural world allow the adult to re-connect. Play and learning becomes an intrinsic, intuitive and shared process that evolves for the child and adult. Uninhibited exploration of the natural elements offers new challenges for the child and 'revisited' challenges for the adult. Child and adult establish a clear sense of individual and collective 'self' as they interact and play together with the elements of the natural world. As child and adult experiment with the forces of particular objects they discover their own strength. The natural play objects stimulate both new ideas and new sensations but also past memories and act as play partners in inquiry between child and adult.

(p. 2)

Research recently carried out (Woods, 2015) supports the interconnectedness between generations and the experience of the outdoor world in particular. Parents attending Little Muddy Boots (a parent and toddler group for under-fives in a large enclosed garden; http://littlemuddyboots.co.uk) were asked 'What are your first memories of outdoor play as a child?' Responses included:

- Large back garden to play in with brothers and sisters with Mum always out there gardening and a nearby disused railway to explore during family dog walks.
- My Dad has always been a huge advocate of outdoor play and designed a garden that included wooden hideaways, aerial runways . . . we were 'playing' outside as a family from kayaking, hiking, cycling, wild swimming, camping etc.
- With cousins at the park.
- Beach, garden with cousins and friends.
- Gardening with Grandma.
- Playing in garden and in street with friends and siblings.
- Building camps, mud pies, traps for siblings; helping my Dad most evenings and weekends in the vegetable garden.

I imagine many of your responses would be similar; the majority of our first experiences of the outside would be with our immediate family and the environmental microsystem of garden, adjacent local areas or family holidays. Having asked students over the years for their earliest memories of childhood, they invariably give answers that reflect playing outside, greatly favouring beach activity, followed by making dens and 'magic potions' with garden ingredients.

The parents were also asked 'What were the reasons for joining Little Muddy Boots?', and second, 'What do you think [your children] have enjoyed most and how do you know this?' They replied:

- I wanted my daughter to learn about nature and learn that getting messy/dirty can be fun.
- To give my children outdoors natural play fostering creativity and love of outdoors; [later response] we often continue activities at home (harvesting, planting, watering, cutting Mr Grass's hair).
- Being amongst other children and muddy play as my son talks about it at home.
- [Second response] yes, we keep things we have made at home to tell other family members about what we have done.
- To enjoy the outdoors together with my daughter in a more structured way; to help her learn and develop; E. also loves taking things she's made home to show Daddy.
- Gain more experiences that are age appropriate for twenty-month-old twins to follow up at home.
- Yes, P. has enjoyed telling his Daddy about muddy boots especially tractor painting.

Here we have a mixture of parents wanting to revisit early memories and the enjoyment of playing outdoors, as well as sharing and relearning gardening habits, and for some, support in developing new skills with their children. I watched story stick making, stick weaving and winding, watering seeds and young plants and harvesting a variety of beans, the parents enjoying this time as much as the children; they were probably less wet and muddy than the little ones' frequent trips between water butt and mud kitchen. Certainly, learning to turn the stiff tap on the water butt was a skill learned by watching, imitating and then developing manipulative skills, the older children as well as the adults helping in this transition. Louv (2012: 144) cites Erickson (n.d.) as saying:

> Research has not looked specifically at a link between outdoor experience and quality of parent–child attachment, and certainly parents can be sensitive and responsive to their babies and young children indoors and out, but in many ways, the natural world seems to invite and facilitate parent–child connection and sensitive interactions.

The activities during the three sessions I participated in was a brief but positive view of high-quality parent–child attachment and mutual involvement. Ryder (pers. comm., 2016) concurs, 'Elemental play invites and facilitates sensitive interactions and adult–child connectedness within the context of the natural world.'

Guided participation

In my experience, the attentiveness and involvement of the parents at Little Muddy Boots was higher than observed at many indoor toddler groups. Rogoff (1990) has looked extensively at cultural tradition and *guided participation* as a means by which children in families within communities pass on knowledge and understanding of roles, vocational habits and tool use. This is a crucial component of elemental play, and for many of the children observed over the years, one that can nurture children's long and close relationship with nature. Where the family and adult practitioner work in harmony, guided participation in shared cultural values becomes a rich resource for the developing child. For Rogoff (in Hall et al., 2008: 60–9)

> guided participation ... refers to the process and systems of involvement between people as they communicate and coordinate efforts while participating in culturally valued activity. Face to face, side by side. 'The guidance' referred to in guided participation involves the direction offered by cultural and social values, as well as social partners; the 'participation' in guided participation refers to observation, as well as hands-on involvement in an activity. The concept of *participatory appropriation* refers to how individuals change through their involvement in one or another activity, in the process of becoming prepared for subsequent involvement in related activities.
>
> [It] includes deliberate attempts to instruct and incidental comments or actions that are overheard or seen as well as involvement with particular materials and experiences that are available, which indicate the direction in which people are encouraged to go or discouraged from going.

She sees

> children's active participation itself as being the process by which they gain facility in an activity. As Wertsch and Stone (1979: 21) put it, 'The process *is* the product.' The participatory appropriation view of how development and learning occur involves a perspective in which children and their social partners are interdependent, their roles are active and dynamically changing, and the specific processes by which they communicate and share in decision making are the substance of cognitive development.
>
> This is different to assimilation or internalisation where a change or new understanding is accommodated with prior learning; it refers to 'the change resulting from a person's *own participation* in an activity'.

We are reminded of Bronfenbrenner's first principle (cited in Vasta, 1992: 206), stating that

> Differences in cognitive performance between groups from different cultures or subcultures are a function of experience, in the course of growing up, with the types of cognitive processes existing in a given culture or subculture at a particular period in its history. Any assessment of the cognitive competence of an individual or group must be interpreted in the light of the culture or subculture in which the person was brought up.

In addition, Rogoff (2003: 71) theorises, 'In our species, each generation comes prepared to learn to participate in the practices and traditions of their elders, aided by shared engagement in values and routine cultural activities'. She later adds (2003: 334):

> Although recent demographic changes seem unprecedented, cultural change and contact among communities have been occurring since the beginning of time. Continual change appears to be a property of living systems, including communities. The changes arise from influences of other communities (whether forced or invited), unforeseen events (desirable or not), and efforts within communities both to maintain traditions and to change in desired directions.

The parents in Little Muddy Boots are a community microcosm where

> The mutual involvement of people working on similar issues is part of the social context of creativity. Dialogue, collaboration, and building from previous approaches often provide the catalyst of putting two ideas together that would not have occurred without the need for the individual thinker to carry out, explain, or improve on an approach.
> (Rogoff, 1990: 199)

What they expressed as enjoyment in childhood with immediate family and friends and older generations, they desire to *afford* their children. The learning they appropriated from grandparents had been assimilated from earlier generations who relied more upon self-sufficiency and agricultural culture. This changing demographic will be explored further in Chapter 3 as I look at the interconnectedness of place and the developing child; the creation of garden groups, forest school and natural environments will be considered in Chapter 8.

In the garden of Little Muddy Boots, it was evident that assimilating the cultural values of growing your own food and how to look after plants was being learned through both informal and formal opportunities, imitation and experience. Children recognised that water from rain was stored in the butt, that seeds and bulbs needed earth to grow, that young plants need water, that beans can be eaten from the plants and this week seeing apples grow in trees in a nearby orchard. There is clearly an environmental and sustainable element to the focus of this toddler group; one which may have taken place in domestic gardens two generations ago, but is perhaps rarer now. May et al. (2006: 13) cite Bruner (1976) as proposing that the passing of knowledge is functional and happens alongside the activity: 'the child was not drawn aside and told how to do it; he was shown while the action was going on'. It may be suggested that elemental play reconceptualises attachment theory to allow for the natural world as a powerful nurturer.

Role of family and community

For any young in a species, the role of parents and the wider family group of carers is one of protection, survival and 'transference of the lores and traditions of a people' (Tuan, 1978: 126). This transference is across all developmental domains: cultural, social, manipulative, behavioural and linguistic. Rogoff (2003: 68) suggests that

> human learning is facilitated by an especially long infancy compared with many other animal species. Many other species are born able to do things that humans cannot, such as walking and feeding themselves. Long infancy may be responsible for our flexibility as a species in learning to use language and other cultural inventions. In this protracted early human development, children can flexibly learn the ways of any community.

Needham (2011: 56) rightly states that 'studies of children's learning from early infancy onwards draw attention to the nature of the interactions between adults and children as a key indicator of effective learning'. Here, he uses a socio-constructivist lens, reflecting Vygotsky's (1978: 56–7) theoretical ideas:

> Every function in the child's cultural development appears twice: first, on the social level, and later, on the individual level; first, *between people (interpsychological)*, and then, *inside* the child (*intrapsychological*). All the higher functions originate as actual relations between human individuals. The transformation of an interpersonal process into an intrapersonal one is the result of a long series of developmental events.
>
> The internalization of socially rooted and historically developed activities is the distinguishing feature of human psychology, the basis of the qualitative leap from animal to human psychology.

Babies and young children, unless their early care is disrupted, form very close attachments to familiar adults; every culture has a different way of offering that care through nuclear or extended families, and through shared care in the wider community. This attachment is acknowledged in the concept of elemental play. As an experienced early years practitioner and keen observer of children welcoming young children into a setting, I have noted that children seem to show a preference, when first arriving each day, to either look for and approach an adult they have formed a close attachment to, or to return to a place in the setting where they feel at ease/enjoy playing or seek the activity/toy/object to continue their schematic play. Sometimes this is more extreme: a child has difficulty separating from a primary carer and will only go to another very familiar adult, sometimes the child's hand is transferred to another hand without apparently breaking physical contact. Staff in settings should be very sensitive to the child/carer relationship and allow for individual and unique separations and watch carefully where and with whom the child is happiest to make their 'transfer'. Winnicott (1971: 135) claimed:

The place where cultural experience is located is in the *potential space* between the individual and the environment (originally the object). For every individual the use of this space is determined by *life experiences* that take place at the early stages of the individual's existence. Every baby has his own favourable or unfavourable experience here. Dependence is maximal. The potential space happens only *in relation to a feeling of confidence* on the part of the baby, that is confidence related to the dependency of the mother-figure or environmental elements, confidence being the evidence of dependability that is becoming introjected.

Socio-constructivism

It is the role of sensitively attuned people to be aware of this overwhelming interest/exploratory drive and to work co-constructively alongside the child. Social connections are made between the child and familiar and attuned people, usually parents and adults working closely with the family dynamic in the community as opportunities are offered that give intimate memories to all involved. The role of key workers has thus been developed, again within an attachment theory framework and can be crucial to a child's well-being, which in turn results in higher involvement with further cognitive, social and emotional activity. McEwan (2015: 11–12) gives insight to a childminder's understanding of a young child and how she is attuned to his experience:

ENCOUNTER: Playing with treasures

Thomas is an eight-month-old baby; he can sit unsupported. He is sitting with a treasure basket containing various objects such as a shell, a metal whisk, wooden balls, keys, corks, wicker coaster, etc. His childminder sits close by observing his play. Thomas picks up a few items and quickly discards them, putting them at the side of the basket. He then tries to pick up the shell but it is too heavy, he looks towards his childminder, who smiles her encouragement and he tries again but it just rolls over. He then turns his attention to the metal whisk. He picks it up and brings it to his mouth, pulls it out, looks at it and then puts it back in his mouth. He drops it and it makes a noise as it hits a metal dish he had already taken out the basket. He smiles and picks up the whisk and bangs it on various items at random. He smiles when the whisk connects with an item that makes a noise. He then brings the whisk once again to his mouth, mouthing it whilst looking around. He then turns his attention to other objects and as he picks out a wooden ball it rolls away, he tracks it with his eyes and then looks towards his childminder and makes a grunt; she acknowledges his sound by saying 'Oh did it roll away, didn't you want that to roll?' He then picks out the whisk once again and continues to explore it in his mouth and by turning it in his hands. After several more minutes play he starts to rub his eyes and make a whining sound, this signals that he has finished, and his childminder acknowledges this and picks him up.

Ryder (2005: 17) argues that relational elements are at the heart of the elemental play philosophy:

> The most important element within this philosophy is the element of *love*, as without it the young children will not interpret joy, wonder, elation etc. This indicates the importance of 'other people' within this play philosophy. Within the element of 'love' the young child learns to interpret their natural world around them as offering them challenges, rather than an environment to be feared.

Vygotsky (1978: 30) has stated:

> From the very first days of the child's development his activities acquire a meaning of their own in a system of social behaviour and, being directed towards a definite purpose, are refracted through the prism of the child's environment. The path from object to child and from child to object passes through another person. This complex human structure is the product of a developmental process deeply rooted in the links between individual and social history.

ENCOUNTER: James' use of natural materials

A couple of weeks ago James, his sister Breanna and their mum, Kathy, went with the under-two teachers, parents and children on a trip to the beach. The reason for the excursion was to collect shells and driftwood to make mobiles to complement our programme which is based on the use of natural and found materials. By the beginning of the next week, Dawn had drilled holes into the driftwood and on the Tuesday I started the process of making a mobile. James (age 1) showed a lot of interest as he picked up the driftwood and explored the shape, length and texture of it. On Wednesday and Thursday mornings, the driftwood and strings were placed on the table and many of the older children would thread up the string. Later on the Thursday, Kathy arrived with Breanna and James and I asked her to help the children tie the knots. A while later, James brought over a large curvy piece of driftwood to me and, interpreting this as a sign to help him make a mobile we found strings and scissors and James watched me thread the string through the hole. I showed James how to pull the string through both the driftwood and shells. James then disappeared and arrived back with Saracen's little blue boot and he smiled when I asked him if he wanted this tied onto the mobile. He then retrieved more driftwood, and two blocks.

I felt he had finished when he no longer brought any further items. He was pleased to have his photograph taken with the mobile. After we had finished we played a beautiful game of 'peek-a-boo' on either side of the door to the outside. Breanna also joined in. But for James it meant much more, because each time that we both put our heads out to say peek-a-boo, we gently touched heads – he and I were both expressing feelings of joy in our great morning together. Lorraine said it was the happiest she has ever seen him.

Ryder (2005) offers an encounter to illustrate the relational context between very young child, adult and *thing*.

Here, elemental play connects materials and experiences in helping James how to recognise that learning is an activity *of* and *for* himself. The natural materials on offer reflect the familiar environment of James (beach and another child's little shoe), invite active exploration of the world beyond the centre and the family and help him recognise his own strengths and power. The sustained shared thinking, here, was active through shared meaning and understanding rather than dialogic: the mobile (the thing of James' interest) took on meaning through *Debbie's mediation*. Gambetti (2003, cited in Thornton and Brunton, 2005: 43) reflects:

> In Reggio we have the highest quality kinds of materials we can find, not so the children can become geniuses but so that they and we have many opportunities to discover their learning processes and their abilities to think. I believe that when you give this to children when they are so young, when you empower them in their thinking, it stays with them forever – as Malaguzzi used to say, like an extra pocket. They understand the power of their intelligence.

The materials and experiences offered by an attuned adult were themselves a means for creative expression and communication for James' thoughts and feelings to another person. This socio-constructivist interpretation illustrates Vygotsky's (1978: 125) theory when he says 'It is in the course of interaction between children and adults that young learners identify effective means for remembering – means made accessible to them by those with more highly developed memory skills.' In a later comment, Ryder (2005) adds that when discussing James' morning with his mum, Kathy, he had started by pointing up to the ceiling. Kathy pieced this information together with having to take the home mobile down as it had become tangled. James had appeared to connect a memory of the mobile at home and the one being constructed at the centre. Debbie had overheard the conversation between James' mum and the centre staff, so was also able to make the connection. Donaldson (1992: 41) is also helpful here:

> infants are specially sensitive to other human beings. That is, within the here/now locus of concern the *focus* of concern is very often relationships with people ... the child's experience of this world is to a large extent mediated by other people; and it is a distinctive thing about our nature of learning is not achieved alone.

James' active and personal exploration and interest in the driftwood became a shared encounter as his memory was exercised and the relationship with Debbie enhanced. Rogoff (2003: 42–52) has researched this experiential and skill-sharing role of attuned and knowledgeable adults further. She notes how 'Margaret Mead's pioneering work demonstrated how passing moments of shared activity, which may or may not have explicit lessons for children, are the material of development' (p. 42). Using tools and involvement in everyday activity within the family or community

> are both inherited and transformed by successive generations. Culture is not static; it is formed from the efforts of people working together, using and adapting material and symbolic tools provided by predecessors and in the process creating new ones.
>
> (p. 51)
>
> Rather than individual development being influenced by (and influencing) culture, from my perspective, people develop as they participate in and contribute to cultural activities that themselves develop with the involvement of people in successive generations. People of each generation, as they engage in sociocultural endeavors with other people, make use of and extend cultural tools and practices inherited from previous generations.
>
> (p. 52)

Socio-culturalism

Elemental play appears to connect socio-cultural ideas and as Bruggeman (1985, cited in Kimes Myers, 1997: 17) suggests, 'that as members of families, caring adults "practice a particular vocation", the creation of a "communal network of memory and hope in which individual members may locate themselves and discern their identities"'. Elemental play is suggestive of cultural memory, where a dividing line between instinctive and learned behaviour is blurred. Hinde (cited in Vasta, 1992: 260–2) suggests that the most important dimensions of socio-cultural and intra-personal interactions fall into eight categories:

- The content of the interactions. (What do the participants do together?)
- The diversity of the interactions. (How many different sorts of things do they do together?)
- The qualities of the several types of interactions.
- Qualities that emerge from the relative frequency and patterning of different types of interaction.
- The complementarity versus reciprocity of the interactions. (Dominant/submissive/synergetic?)
- Intimacy. (Do they reveal themselves to each other?)
- Interpersonal perception. (Do they see each other as they really are? Do they understand each other? Do they feel understood?)
- Commitment. (Do they strive to continue the relationship or to improve its properties?)

More recently, Waters (2014: 103) questions the aspects of a space which also relates to the socio-cultural relationship

> 'What can I do here? What's in this space? Who's in this space with me?' and 'How do we behave here? What are the cultural rules between these people and this space?' These interactions are culturally specific, evolving and dynamic; *'human learning presupposes a specific social nature by which children grow into the intellectual life of those around them'* (Vygotsky, 1978: 88).

Rogoff (2003: 58) is again helpful:

> Together, the interpersonal, personal and cultural-institutional aspects of [an] event constitute the activity. No aspect exists or can be studied in isolation from the others. An observer's relative focus on one or the other aspect can be changed, but they do not exist apart from each other. Analysis of interpersonal arrangements could not occur without background understanding of community processes (such as the historical and cultural roles and changing practices of [. . .] families.

Using an elemental play lens helps us to unify our observation of relationships between adults and children and the environments they dynamically inhabit; the environments change over time as the dependence of the child lessens through developing maturity. Tuan (1977: 138) concurs, 'To the young child the parent is his primary "place". The caring adult is for him a source of nurture and a haven of stability. The adult is also the guarantor of meaning to the child, for whom the world can often seem baffling.' It is to the 'baffling' exploration of place that we turn to in Chapter 3.

Provocations

- What stimulates the adult to want to mediate the child's learning process with the natural elements?
- Where and when might we talk more about the learning process using natural elements?
- In what ways can someone demonstrate a 'natural' disposition?
- Why do some adults affiliate more easily than others with this concept of mediating children's learning in relation to the natural world? What are their early experiences?
- How often are they being provided an opportunity by working with very young children in a natural context to revisit their own early experiences in nature? Can you find evidence of this in your planning or experiential learning?

- Is it more about 'experience' than 'memories'? Is there any difference?
- Do you have to 'remember' the experience or do you just need to have experienced it and it comes back to you?
- Where do you feel most comfortable playing with young children?
- Where can we extend children's independent but supported knowledge of environment and habitat?

References

Bjorkland, D.F. and Pellegrini, A.D. (2002) *The Origins of Human Nature. Evolutionary Developmental Psychology*. Washington, DC: American Psychological Association.

Bronfenbrenner, U. (1979) *The Ecology of Human Development. Experiments by Nature and Design*. Cambridge, MA: Harvard University Press.

Donaldson, M. (1992) *Human Minds. An Exploration*. London: Penguin.

Hall, K., Murphy, P. and Soler, J. (eds) (2008) *Pedagogy and Practice: Culture and Identities*. Milton Keynes: Open University Press.

Kahn, Jr. P.H. and Kellert, S.R. (eds) (2002) *Children and Nature. Psychological, Sociocultural and Evolutionary Investigations*. Cambridge, MA: MIT Press.

Kimes Myers, B. (1997) *Young Children and Spirituality*. London: Routledge.

Louv, R. (2012) *The Nature Principle. Reconnecting with Life in a Virtual Age*. Chapel Hill, NC: Algonquin.

May, P., Ashford, E. and Bottle, G., (2006) *Sound Beginnings: Learning and Development in the Early Years*. London: David Fulton.

McEwan, V. (2015) Children are naturally playful. In A. Woods (ed.) *The Characteristics of Effective Learning. Creating and Capturing the Possibilities in the Early Years*. London: David Fulton, pp. 8–22.

Mills, J. (2006) Elemental play: Exploring a notion of socio cultural adult/child play that links intuitive connections with nature with a holistic approach to development. Unpublished MA thesis, Sheffield University.

Ministry of Education (1996) *Te Whāriki*. Wellington, NZ: Learning Media.

Needham, M. (2011) Using activity theory to examine the factors shaping the learning partnership in a parent and child 'stay and play' session. In T. Waller, J. Whitmarsh and K. Clarke (eds) *Making Sense of Theory and Practice in Early Childhood*. Maidenhead: McGraw Hill/Open University Press, pp. 54–68.

Rogoff, B. (1990) *Apprenticeship in Thinking. Cognitive Development in Social Context*. Oxford: Oxford University Press.

Rogoff, B. (2003) *The Cultural Nature of Human Development*. Oxford: Oxford University Press.

Ryder, D. (2005) *Elemental Play: More than Sand and Water.* Unpublished.

Thornton, L. and Brunton, P. (2005) *Understanding the Reggio Approach.* London: David Fulton.

Tuan, Y.-F. (1977) *Space and Place. The Perspective of Experience.* Minneapolis, MN: University of Minnesota Press.

Tuan, Y.-F. (1978) Children and the natural environment. In I. Altman and J.F. Wohlwill (eds) *Human Behaviour and Environment, Advances in Theory and Research. Vol. 3: Children and the Environment.* New York: Plenum Press, pp. 5–32.

Vasta, R. (ed.) (1992) *Six Theories of Child Development: Revised Formulations and Current Issues.* London: Jessica Kingsley.

Vygotsky, L.S. (1978) *Mind in Society. The Development of Higher Psychological Processes.* Cambridge, MA: Harvard University Press.

Waller, T. (ed.) (2009) *An Introduction to Early Childhood.* London: Sage.

Waters, J. (2014) Getting the most out of outdoor spaces. In T. Maynard and J. Waters (eds) *Exploring Outdoor Play in the Early Years.* Maidenhead: Oxford University Press, pp. 98–111.

Winnicott, D. (1971) *Playing and Reality.* London and New York: Routledge.

CHAPTER 3

Exploring the outdoor world with others

Holt (1970: 101) describes

> The courage of little children (and not them alone) rises and falls, like the tide – only the cycles are in minutes, or even seconds. We can see this vividly when we watch infants of two or so, walking with their mothers, or playing in a playground or park. Not long ago I saw this scene in the Public Garden in Boston. The mothers were chatting on a bench while the children roamed around. For a while they would explore boldly and freely, ignoring their mothers. Then, after a while, they would use up their store of courage and confidence, and run back to their mothers' sides, and cling there for a while, as if to recharge their batteries. After a moment or two of this they were ready for more exploring, and so they went out, then came back, and then ventured out again.

The premise presented in this book is that children are born with a disposition for elemental play, an affinity with nature and the elemental components of the world that humans have evolved in. Further, that elemental play may explain the exploratory activity of young children as they discover, seek, accept and reject both natural and found materials through nurturing and reciprocal relationships with adults whose role is to welcome them into the cultural world around them.

Heerwagen and Orians (2002: 29) argue that

> The developmental psychological literature focuses on how changes in childhood are influenced by the combination of children's experience and the sociocultural environment. However, a full understanding of these changes also requires consideration of the physical and biological environments encountered by children and of our evolutionary history.

Let's take Alfie as an example.

> **ENCOUNTER: Alfie**
>
> Alfie digging and digging and digging – a big hole near the scrubby bushes to see what he could find – particularly dinosaur bones.
>
> Alfie always turning up at nursery with scabby knees, muddy hands and toenails, usually on his bike which, at four years old, he showed good balance, competence and skill.
>
> Alfie knowing the names of many plants and types of rock.
>
> Alfie bringing his hen to nursery one day.
>
> How might we interpret Alfie's dispositions and constant play behaviours?

According to Gardner (2006), he could be demonstrating the eighth intelligence: naturalistic. He certainly shows a strong, environmental awareness and prefers to play outdoors over and above any activity inside the nursery, unless it was to fashion a tool he needed or to look at a book of dinosaurs. Alfie also worked on the allotments with his mum, played in his dad's building restoration workshop and regularly visited Robin Hood Bay to find fossils.

Verbeek and de Waal (2002: 8) would also suggest that 'Human developmental research inspired by the influential developmentalist and biologist Jean Piaget portrays childhood as a period during which we are particularly motivated to seek out the natural world around us. Shepard (1983) refers to this process as "loading the ark".'

Exploratory motivation

Using the elemental play model, Alfie is at the centre, fully attuned to following his own projects and ideas through the nested and contextual relationships with his parents, who themselves have an elevated connection to exploring and to building activities with natural materials. Alfie, at four, was not yet ready to write, was not interested in computers or any passive activity but was an adventurer, 'ark-loader', explorer, problem-solver and leader in risky, outdoor play.

Without exception, young children I have watched, played with and observed in woods, gardens, and playgrounds and on beaches have dug, scraped, hidden, draped, revisited and returned to this scavenger-type behaviour. I did it and I expect you did it too.

Very recently, Finn, another two year old in the garden, wanted to add stones to the sand in the shallow tray and picked up a pot to collect the gravel we had just crunched through – he was attracted to the sound. The first time, we filled the pot to the top, but in every subsequent trot down the path, he only put one stone in, carried it, emptied it and started all over again. Ava and Finn will not be the only children who collect and transport in this way, the process appearing more

> **ENCOUNTER: Teachers in school**
>
> 1. Visiting a trainee, the class teacher talked about the development of the outdoor space and how they had put a safety surface, some plastic climbing and the house equipment on the site but found that the children seemed more drawn to the loose gravel path, constantly picking up, scraping and collecting up the gravel in the buckets 'which were for the sand tray'.
> 2. Existing slide in playground had a platform underneath. The majority of children used the platform with cushions, rather than the slide, to create a sheltered space for playing and reading.
> 3. Running round and hiding in the boundary hedges seemed to attract children rather than the expensive wooden fort erected on the grass; lots of toys and treasures were found daily under the bushes.

> **ENCOUNTER: Ava**
>
> Ava is in my garden with her parents; she is seventeen months old. I have set out a shallow tray with sand and pots. She plays for a while, filling and emptying pots, squashing mounds and then turns to a book. She points to and recognises a ball – trying to sound out 'ball' and we go to the garage to fetch a ball. On the way back, we walk along the gravel drive and she crouches to pick up a few stones, carrying them back to the sand tray. She takes a pot, goes back to the drive alone and fills the pot, bringing it back when full. This 'game' lasts for forty-five minutes.
>
> Is it a transporting schema? Is it the availability of loose materials? Is it collecting natural resources because they feel and look interesting? Is it because she feels an affinity with an element?

important than the product. After repeating this 'fetch and carry' for around fifteen minutes, he appeared content to leave the activity and move on to another area in the garden:

> The neural processes that guided our ancestors' behaviours in Pleistocene hunting and gathering bands are likely to still be in operation today (Pinker, 1997; Cosmides & Tooby; 1993). These mechanisms have been designed by evolution to guide adaptive responses to enduring ecological challenges – such as distinguishing edible from inedible foods, avoiding encounters with dangerous animals, avoiding dangerous con-specifics, finding the way home, avoiding inanimate hazards, and finding a place to live.
>
> (Heerwagen and Orians, 2002: 35)

Anthropologically, humans have evolved due to their exploration, dexterity, imagination, problem-solving and community activities and I believe that what we see very young children doing is reflecting early human development. The memory of this early development can be argued to have become a cultural and environmental memory passed down through generations by learnt and species-innate behaviour: 'Elemental play acknowledges latent "hunter/gatherer" tendencies that are still apparent in young children and celebrates it as an essential ecological and developmental experience' (Ryder, pers. comm., 2016).

Sanders (2009: 60) has argued:

> From a Darwinian perspective, it could be argued that one reason human societies differ from each other in the first place is that the world consists of tropical rain forests, vast plains, mountainous areas, deserts, areas of permafrost, and so forth. Culture is perhaps largely a reflection that human species have been compelled to adapt to different environments, thereby reflecting a diversity at least as wide-ranging as the ecological niches within which people are born, grow, live and die.

Evolution

Young children's adaptation to the world they are born into is very much part of the elemental play model. The phrase 'ecological niches' was first used by Bronfenbrenner. Vasta (1992: 192–4) refers to Bronfenbrenner who states that

> particular environmental conditions have been shown to produce different developmental consequences depending on the personal characteristics of individuals living in that environment.
>
> ... there needs to be a consideration of the *processes* through which characteristics of person, environment, or of both together, can influence human development.
>
> The 'person-context model' – The particular strength of person-context design lies in their capacity to identify what I call *ecological niches. These are particular regions in the environment that are especially favourable or unfavourable to the development of individuals with particular personal characteristics.*

Robinson's original concept (1977: 22–3) stated:

> genetically, we are all hunter-gatherers. Cultural transmission: the set of processes by which each new generation of human beings, in any social group, acquires and builds upon the skills, knowledge, lore, and values – that is the culture – of previous generations in that group.

This is echoed by Bjorkland and Pellegrini (2002: 193–6) who say:

Evolution of the human species' unique intelligence was motivated by the need to deal with other members of our social group. Although social learning is observed in many other primate species, only humans possess *cultural learning* – the transmission of acquired information and behaviour within and across generations with a high degree of fidelity.

Griffiths (2013) reiterates:

> every generation of children instinctively nests itself in nature, no matter how tiny a scrap of it they can grasp.
>
> (p. 2)

> human nature is nested in nature which co-creates the child.
>
> (p. 7)

> [and] for years of evolutionary history, children have trapped, grown, found, hunted or fished for themselves and cooked on their own fires.
>
> (p. 46)

Gray (2013: 22–4, 26) a contemporary of Griffiths also writes that 'education is cultural transmission . . . symbolised by trustful parenting'.

We develop within the social and environmental context of our 'home-place' or landscape, and we adapt to its qualities, boundaries and cultural norms. We are kept warm and safe and as young children are nourished and nurtured in order to develop into tomorrow's adults, taking their place in the world to parent the next generation. Survival is paramount and risk-taking an everyday response to natural encounters with the world where we learn to adapt and take care of ourselves, others and the many co-species we meet. This is sometimes called 'heft' by farmers long established on pieces of land where they develop a deep and rich understanding of the behaviours of the earth, the weather, the crops, the contours and the animals who can thrive.

In much of the western world, this will not entail hunting for our own food, lighting fires for warmth and moving as nomads to follow weather patterns, animal movements or crop-growing:

> Children have reducing opportunities to understand their 'place in nature'. Rivkin (1997) comments that the development of humans from a species in largely natural environments to a mostly indoor existence is so recent that most adults still remember outdoor play as a significant and treasured part of their childhood.
>
> (Davis and Elliott, 2003: 8)

Generational echoes

In a small, informal research project (2015) at Little Muddy Boots, responses from parents about their first memories included:

- building a bonfire for bonfire night;
- finding ladybirds and blackberry picking;
- in the surrounding area of fields;
- building camps and mud pies;
- playing in the woods, woodland walks;
- beach and garden;
- losing wellies in the mud;
- splashing in a stream.

For those of us with a deeply held commitment to outdoor play, it is more than nostalgia that guides us in affording very young children with similar natural play experiences:

> Research has yet to show how childhood experiences develop environmental values. Nevertheless, there are growing indications that such values are rooted in childhood environmental experiences (Rivkin, 1997), and that groundings are set for children to learn to become 'environmental activists' later in life, as a result of their early experiences. A study by Chawla (1998) of adult environmental activists identified significant childhood environmental experiences as precursors to their adult activism.
>
> (Davis and Elliott, 2003: 7)

Wattchow and Brown (2011: 4) concur:

> Significant life experience research into the formative experiences of environmental educators indicates that many of the elements present in my own childhood (family interest, regular visits to a 'natural' place, access to environmental literature) are all key indicators in the development of an interest in environmental education and activism.

Titman (1994: 19) has written extensively about the development of school grounds and children's favourite places and preferred designs for outdoor places and has this to add to our collective memories of early experience with nature:

> Memories of exciting places characterized by intense experience rather than repetitive [. . .] outdoor places were remembered out of all proportion to the relative number of hours spent there. In relation to transcendence, [Chawla] notes that freedom and a natural environment were almost invariable

factors and that the opportunity to consider the environment one's own, to touch and explore without fear of transgression, was essential. Affection was always associated with places that were valued by the adults around the child as well as by the child itself, and involved exploration and discovery in places that children appropriated as their own. Chawla explains the difference between affection and transcendence as involving the '*social embeddedness of the place*'. [my italics]

Chawla finds that physical factors alone were insufficient as determinants of environmental memory because social, cultural and personal factors were equally significant and that a key element for children relates to the extent to which places engender a sense of belonging. This work suggests that the 'semiotics' of places, the messages and meanings which are conveyed, are very influential in terms of the significance of environmental experience in childhood.

Tuan (1977: 154, 159) also comments:

> This profound attachment to the homeland appears to be a worldwide phenomenon. It is known to literate and non-literate peoples, hunter-gatherers, and sedentary farmers as well as city dwellers. The city or land is viewed as mother, and it nourishes; place is an archive of fond memories and splendid achievements that inspire the present; place is permanent and hence reassuring to man, who sees frailty in himself and chance and flux everywhere.
>
> Attachment of a deep though subconscious sort may come simply with familiarity and ease, with the assurance of nurture and security, with the memory of sounds and smells, of communal activities and homely pleasures accumulated over time.

Landscape

Elemental play suggests it is in the exploration of 'What can I do in this place?', 'What does this place afford me to do?' and a feeling of 'belonging to a place' that helps explain feeling at home on earth. It is a process of finding out about the self in relation to people, places and things in *my landscape*. As has been previously explored in Chapter 2, for many children, their observed attachment is to people, and settling a child making the transition from primary carer to community carer is generally supported through key workers and familiar adults. For some children, the security of a familiar place is paramount. Ryder (2005: 3) was able to identify the needs and interests of a particular child in this respect in the Encounter with Kian on the following page.

In Chapter 5, relationships with the earth's elements will be discussed in further detail but it is difficult to deny the excitement we observe in young children when they are playfully absorbed in mud, water, sand, wood, leaves, sticks and clay. Children afforded the possibilities of immersion in the outdoor world with adults

> **ENCOUNTER: Kian**
>
> I had identified the interest of a particular child in the way he needed to be outside to settle before his mum would leave. I was soon to learn a very important factor when working with infants and toddlers – flexibility of routines. Even though this child arrived at lunchtime when the door was shut, I needed to reflect on this practice, and therefore, for this particular child it meant that I opened the door and allowed him to settle outside. He was happy and his mum was happy. We were later to discover that we had such a strong belief in our infants and toddlers as competent children that the door to outside was eventually left open at lunchtime and none of the children left the food table until they had finished.

who are modelling the enjoyment, engagement and environmental respect for finite natural resources are, it is suggested, nurturing a past, present and future interdependent relationship with the planet that nourishes us. Moore and Cosco (2003: 1) remind us that

> From the day they are born, children must begin learning the most important truth that the biosphere is our sole source of life support: air, water, sunlight, materials to construct shelter from climactic extremes, fire for heating and cooking, and soil for growing food.

'It seems reasonable to conclude that experience of the natural environment is one of the crucial continuities in human life, giving adults a recollected 'grounding' in their childhood years' (Moore and Young, 1978: 111).

Freddie is at a forest school. He is looking after insects found in the environment. He has a notion of shelter and natural materials. He can use appropriate tools for the problem he has encountered. He recognises that ladybirds live in the woods and is displaying a sense of co-relationship and belonging in the woods. Some children always look for the snails; others have a 'lying tree', one that is of sufficient challenge but within their skill level to climb into and lie across the branches. Older children show the new ones where the rabbit droppings can be found, and others return to a small pine tree that gives up cones for them to collect.

In both encounters, the children discovered other species in the environment of the forest school – a small and immature woodland, surrounded by fields, public footpaths and fencing. There are birds, rabbits, insects, cows and evidence of other animals which children delight in examining and comparing – fox/dog and badger poo with cow-pats, for example. They look at the berries that the animals eat and find apples and pears from a few fruit trees planted in the woods. They find sticks and boughs for shelters and delight in the puddles that form and disappear in different weathers. They descend into a small stream when the water is shallow

ENCOUNTER: Freddie

Freddie has spent some minutes finding ladybirds with his friend Josh. It has been a bright day in late spring and the ladybirds have emerged to enjoy the sunshine. The boys have been counting both the number of ladybirds and their spots. Josh runs off to join more boisterous play in the woods and Freddie sits still whilst a ladybird climbs onto his hand, up his sleeve and across his chest before descending the zip on his jacket. Freddie is very patient and is talking quietly to the ladybird. He sits for around twenty minutes. He asks me why there are so many ladybirds in the woods today and wonders where they have been living as no 'houses' seem obvious. We talk about spaces where ladybirds go to seek warmth and shelter and I tell him about the sash windows in my house that seem to shelter many of them. The following week, Freddie looks for ladybirds again – there are fewer – and he wonders whether it is too cold and damp for them and thinks aloud about making a shelter. He looks at the shelter we had made with tree boughs and begins to collect sticks. Looking at them, he realizes the comparative height of sticks to the ladybirds and sees a problem. He thinks they need to be smaller so I give him a pair of secateurs to use. He estimates the length he needs and spends forty-five minutes cutting the sticks to pretty much equal size, planting them upright into the ground so that the ladybirds can shelter in the rain that feels inevitable on this damper morning in the woods.

ENCOUNTER: In the field

On my last visit, the group of children took a perimeter walk along the adjacent field. There were many cows loudly mooing as the farmer was feeding them from a tractor. The children started shouting 'cow' and the cows seemed to them to be responding with 'moo'! On the way back from the corner of the field, the eight children spontaneously climbed to the top of a large metal gate, hanging on the top rail and again started shouting 'cow'; by now the cows were wandering off. The children began singing, without any prompting: 'Old MacDonald', 'Bouncing on a Tractor' and 'Baa Baa Black Sheep'. The Forest Leader said this was not something other children had done but this group seemed to have developed an ownership of this gate and the conversation/singing to the cows.

and look for the different insect habitats in the shade of this stream. They are the experiences that we as adults will recall, and as Shepard (1983) has said, have afforded the possibility of 'loading the ark', or as Chawla (1990: 19, cited in Elliott and Davis, 2004) describes 'radioactive jewels buried within us, emitting energy across the years of our life'. Chawla later (2006: 70–1) points out:

No two crickets, no two rotting logs, no stream, pool or puddle, no bank of earth is ever the same. It is the world in which human beings evolved, with which children have a connection as ancient as the chemistry of their cells. It is the world for which they are adapted, on which human existence depends. Nature's newness is composed of established elements and patterns. In processes of joint attention, the social and physical realms function together. People around a child foster a bond with nature not only by giving the child freedom to move about and engage autonomously with natural areas but also by their own example.

'My' places

Children's pattern of behaviours remind us of Moore and Young's (1978: 121–2) suggestion that

> Children-only routes were places to 'dilly-dally on the way'; exploration-for-its-own-sake. Routes are 'ritualized' by groups of friends.
>
> Inevitably, the most significant places occur at the intersections of many behaviour settings, where the inherent potential of elements and attributes coincide with behavioural competencies of the majority of users. In complex landscapes, pathways and places are so thickly spread on the ground that they form a pyramid of overlapping schemata and interdependent behaviours. Such *multipurposeness* (the capacity of a place to accommodate a variety of activities simultaneously or in sequence) is usually the result of deliberate design, although it may sometimes arise from serendipitous combinations of natural and cultural forces, as in an old rural cemetery. This kind of juxtaposition provides a powerful stimulus for children, drawing them beyond their habitual domain, into a perceptually more boundless 'as if' world where mind, body, and landscape can be in more fluid contact. A conclusion that stands out is the evident cultural dependency of children's outdoor relationships. The impression is strong enough to suggest that every subculture has a significant ethos in childhood environmental experience (Young, 1975). Interrelated with cultural dependencies there also exist, theoretically, more universal species-specific developmental functions, facilitated or constrained as a result of children's outdoor experience.

Certainly, a group of children meeting in this forest school a couple of years ago were 'boundary markers'. Their 'group' activity was keen to walk the perimeter regularly. This was a summer period; the grasses and nettles were taller than the children, like a jungle, and it was almost as if the children wanted to *master* this environment. The grasses were to be explored and conquered, never mind that they could not see far, but singing and calling reminded them of the presence of their friends and that the walk, once learned, would lead them back to 'the tree'. Sometimes they dragged a long, long stick, other times they dilly-dallied when finding a butterfly or snail. One is reminded of tribal and nomadic movements through long, savannah grasses and wooded areas of terrain looking for shelter and food. Orr (2005: 91) reinforces Bronfenbrenner's ecological systems theory when he explains:

> Places are laboratories of diversity and complexity, mixing social functions and natural processes. A place has a human history and a geologic past; it is part of an eco-system with a variety of Microsystems, it is a landscape with particular flora and fauna. Its inhabitants are part of a social, economic, and political order; they are linked by innumerable bonds to other places. It can be understood only on its terms as a complex mosaic of phenomena and problems.

Exploring new and familiar environments

It seems that each group of children, and indeed family, enjoy, re-create, navigate and create new pathways for themselves in environments where they feel secure and keen to explore. Ouvrey (2000: 12) claims that

> Young children learn about themselves and their environment through movement. Jean Piaget, Jerome Bruner and Margaret Donaldson – great and influential developmental psychologists – say that for our youngest children, movement is 'thought in action'. Children have first to experience the world actively through all their senses before they can think in the abstract and hold thoughts or the memory of those things in their heads as pictures, concepts or symbols.

Many of our earliest memories are evoked not just by landscapes and terrain, but also the feel and smell of places such as the beach or a woodland or of an activity in a special place like a bonfire. Whenever I pick blackcurrants, then transport them back to the kitchen in a metal colander and prepare them for jam-making in my apron, I become *my* grandmother in her kitchen fifty years ago with her larder full of stores, the penetrating smell of blackcurrants and the permission to pick and eat as many loganberries from the garden as I liked. When walking in a formal garden, I am transported back to the neat borders of flowers in my grandfather's garden, the hen coops and their tabby cat, another grandmother singing. Titman (1994: 20) again reminds us:

> Relph (1976) explains existential insidedness as the 'inner structure of space as it appears to us in our concrete experience of the world as members of a cultural group' ... we form judgements about places; who they are for or belong to; whether they can be 'owned'; whether they are places 'for me' or 'people like me'; and what we can do in and with them.

> Proshansky and Fabian (1987) describe place identity as the 'physical-world socialisation of the child'. They suggest that place identity is 'a substructure of the person's self-identity that is comprised of cognitions about the physical environment that also serve to define who the person is' . . . children look at the environment in terms of its physical and social meanings in order to understand their surroundings, to satisfy their needs and in so doing learn to behave appropriately. They believe that the ability to 'read' environments and to form concepts about place-identity is essential to a child's development of a sense of competence and control of the physical world, which is in turn an important aspect of self-identity.

And having recently become a grandmother, I, too, wish to establish a place where my granddaughter will develop a sense of belonging; where smells and textures, sounds and experiences will be in her 'ark' and, like Malaguzzi, I can be nostalgic for her future where her encounters will evoke similar memories of being a granddaughter. Abelman (2005: 182–3) provokes in us a deeper sense of place:

> Now I have a second son. Every evening we wrap him in his favourite wool blanket and ever so slowly walk the length of the farm saying good night to the chickens, touching the leaves on the asparagus, rubbing our faces on various herbs and flowers, and quietly sneaking up on the thousands of frogs that inhabit our pond. It's the same route each evening, but every walk reveals something new. Most nights just as we reach the farm-gate and turn to walk back home young Benjamin's eyes have started to close as he is lulled and calmed by the life on the farm, which is also drifting into sleep. These walks include no talk, no explanations; there is no reading or study required to understand and learn from our experience. But I am sure that young B. is absorbing it all, even when his eyes are closed and he is asleep.
>
> On, our first walk out at ten days old, I pointed out the squirrels, the colours of the autumn trees, and the smell of the fallen leaves to my granddaughter. She was cosy and asleep . . . but we will walk this way again.

Tuan (1977: 199) understands this, 'Human beings, like other animals, feel at home on earth. Learning is rarely at the level of explicit and formal instruction: distance, landmarks, [and] routes.' Children naming a tree, children owning a park, children roaming and finding their way back to adults or friends, children secure in walking to school or a friend's house and children creating their own spaces in gardens, parks, playgrounds and rooms. Children make locational as well as functional places, much as their parents and generations of children before them. Places are important: the preschool cloakroom where a little three year old sat and refused to take his coat off because that was where his mum had left him, and confidently he expected her to return. The home-corner in the nursery where yesterday's play scenario could be re-joined. The dip at the edge of the playing field that shielded us from prying eyes where we could stable our 'horses' and create stories. The open space in the woodland where shelters were erected and the base tree identified. These are locations, coupled with imagination, emotion, exploration, and security-behaviours evolved through cultural contexts.

Nabhan and St Antoine (1993: 229–30) speculate:

> Perhaps biophilia is not genetically determined but is a set of learned responses; or it could be a set of behaviours based on a number of genes, for which any particular individual may have some but not all of the genes . . . some human genetic lineages may have been selected for biophilic responses more than others . . . consistent with Wilson's original hypothesis, is that a child's learning environment greatly conditions the expression of any genetic basis for biophilia. Unless the appropriate environmental triggers are present in a certain cultural/environmental context, biophilia is unlikely to be fully expressed.

Moore and Young (1978: 119–20) suggest that

> Place-making may result from small modifications to fixed resources, a 'fort' for instance may exist as an almost imperceptible depression in long grass. As children move through the environment, they may scratch the dirt, pick a couple of mottled stones from the edge of the highway, pluck a few flower heads to decorate their person, or discover some latent play function in the detritus of modern life.

Hart (1977) recorded that children spent a large amount of time building places for themselves, and observed that many of the 'houses' of children under eight were 'found' places with scarcely any major physical modification. They nevertheless served the users well, who modified and differentiated their interiors via their imaginations, rather than by hand. He concluded that a requirement of building activity was a 'flexible landscape' to ensure a ready supply of 'loose parts'. Nicholson's (1971) loose parts theory will be discussed further in later chapters, suffice to say that the availability of loose parts for building and shelter would have been essential concerns for hunter-gatherer communities.

Places that have meaning

Davis and Elliott (2003: 7) suggest

> That early childhood education has a vital role in creating pro-environment attitudes and values. This means learning about and embracing the values, concepts and practices that underpin sustainability and tasks that are perhaps not as daunting as they first might seem. Early childhood education already has the foundations for embedding sustainability into its philosophies, theories and practices, but these are largely unrecognized. These relate, first, to the

already existing focus on social justice and human rights in early childhood curriculum, and second, to long-held beliefs and practices which support children's interactions with nature.

Ryder's encounter earlier in the chapter, demonstrates an understanding and empathy towards the elemental play model which both encompasses a belief in reciprocal relationships with people, places and things but is also deeply embedded with pro-environment values and practice. Tuan (1978: 7) states that 'Environmentalism is the belief that nature affects human beings and their institutions', with Moore and Young (1987: 123) further suggesting that 'under appropriate ecological conditions children themselves will reveal environmental dependencies that lie beyond the conditioning effects of the particular culture they were born into'. Moore and Cosco, (2003) concur with many current early years practitioners when they suggest

> A small but growing body of research indicates that daily experience of nature, spending time outdoors in the fresh air and sunlight, in touch with plants and animals, has a measurable impact on healthy child development. Children have a right to develop in an environment that stimulates their healthy development as mandated by the UN Convention on the Rights of the Child. To fulfill this mandate, nature must be seen as an essential component of the experiential world of childhood, designed into every childhood habitat, providing daily immersion in nature, putting children in close touch with the biosphere.

There does appear to be a renewed and growing interest in providing outdoor experiences for young children. One might argue this is in response to concerns about the level of physical activities that children are engaged in; it may also reflect a particular view of many early years practitioners who *aim*

> to revolutionise early education in the UK. Our children are incredibly creative and resourceful, and they don't get bored. They can make up a game with a couple of sticks. They are only restricted by their minds not their environment. Parents are blown away when they come to see the nursery, saying it's so beautiful. But I always say it's not rocket science, it's just children playing outside and our role is resisting the urge to direct and overstimulate them.
>
> (Barrett, cited in Gaunt, 2016)

The connectedness of the idea of elemental play, growth in forest schools, 'nomadic settings', research and eco-psychological ideology from Canada and the United States of America, the approaches of Reggio Emilia, Scandinavian friluftsliv and Te Whāriki suggests a more persuasive philosophy and, although I am hesitant to suggest this, perhaps a nostalgia for a kinder, more spiritual life in the face of global tensions, environmental concerns and demographic change. In the next chapter, it is spiritual awareness that is further explored.

Provocations

- Tuan (1978: 30) asks: In what ways can a natural setting affect the perceptual and conceptual development of the child?
- Kahn and Kellert (2003: vii) ask: What are the evolutionary origins of children's relationships with nature?
- Children's direct experience with nature is straightforward to describe and explain; indirect experience involves more restricted contexts such as visits to zoos, arboretums or aquariums or perhaps encounters with domestic animals at home. Vicarious experiences can be described as encounters with symbolic representations of the natural world through film, books and computers. Consider the balance of experiences in your setting and in what ways direct encounters could be increased.
- Wattchow and Brown (2011: 71) suggest we ask children: 'What has happened [in this place]? Who has lived here? How have they lived here? What seems to be happening in this place now? How often do you incorporate environmental and philosophical questions into your daily practice?
- Where are the places inside and outside in your setting that children return to again and again? Reflect on the qualities of these places.

References

Abelman, M. (2005) Raising whole children is like raising good food: beyond factory farming and factory schooling. In M.K. Stone and Z. Barlow (eds) *Ecological Literacy. Educating Our Children for a Sustainable World*. San Francisco: Sierra Club Books, pp. 175–83.

Bjorkland, D.F. and Pellegrini, A.D. (2002) *The Origins of Human Nature. Evolutionary Developmental Psychology*. Washington, DC: American Psychological Association.

Chawla, L. (2006) Learning to love the world enough to protect it. www.ntnu.no/documents/10458/19133135/Chawla1.pdf (accessed 14 September 2015).

Davis, J. and Elliott, S. (2003) *Early Childhood Environmental Education. Making it Mainstream*. Canberra: Early Childhood Australia.

Elliott, S. and Davis, J. (2004) Mud pies and daisy chains: connecting young children and nature. *Every Child* 10(4): 4–5.

Gardner, H. (2006) *The Development and Education of the Mind. The Selected Works of Howard Gardner*. London and New York: Routledge.

Gaunt, C. (2016) Outdoor and forest school nurseries expand across London. *Nursery World*, 11 March. www.nurseryworld.co.uk/nursery-world/news/1156379/outdoor-and-forest-school-nurseries-expand-across-london (accessed 13 March 2016).

Gray, P. (2013) *Free to Learn. Why Unleashing the Instinct to Play Will Make Our Children Happier, More Self-Reliant and Better Students for Life*. New York: Basic Books.

Griffiths, J. (2013) *Kith. The Riddle of the Childscape*. London: Hamish Hamilton.

Hart, T. (2003) *The Secret Spiritual World of Children*. Makawao, HI: Inner Ocean.

Heerwagen, J.H. and Orians, G.H. (2002) The ecological world of children, In P.H. Kahn, Jr. and S.R. Kellert (eds) *Children and Nature. Psychological, Sociocultural and Evolutionary Investigations*. Cambridge, MA: MIT Press, pp. 29–64.

Holt, J. (1970) *How Children Learn*. London: Penguin.

Kahn, Jr. P.H. and Kellert, S.R. (2002) Introduction. In P.H. Kahn, Jr. and S.R. Kellert (eds) *Children and Nature. Psychological, Sociocultural and Evolutionary Investigations*. Cambridge, MA: MIT Press.

Moore, R.C. and Cosco, N.G. (2003) Developing an earth-bound culture through design of childhood habitats. www.naturallearning.org/earthboundpaper.html (accessed 19 March 2006).

Moore, R. and Young, D. (1978) Childhood outdoors: towards a social ecology of the landscape. In I. Altman and J.F. Wohlwill (eds) *Human Behaviour and Environment, Advances in Theory and Research. Vol. 3: Children and the Environment*. New York: Plenum Press, pp. 83–130.

Nabhan, G.P. and St Antoine, S. (1993) The loss of floral and faunal story: the extinction of experience. In S.R. Kellert and E.O. Wilson (eds) *The Biophilia Hypothesis*. Washington, DC: Island Press.

Orr, D.W. (2005) Place and pedagogy. In M.K. Stone and Z. Barlow (eds) *Ecological Literacy. Educating Our Children for a Sustainable World*. San Francisco: Sierra Club Books, pp. 85–95.

Ouvrey, M. (2000) *Exercising Muscles and Minds*. London: National Early Years Network.

Robinson, E. (1977) *A Study of the Religious Experience of Childhood*. Oxford: Religious Education Centre.

Ryder, D. (2005) Elemental play: more than sand and water. Unpublished.

Sanders, B. (2009) Childhood in different cultures. In T. Maynard and T. Thomas (eds) *An Introduction to Early Childhood Studies*, 2nd edn. London: Sage, pp. 53–64.

Titman, W. (1994) Special places; special people. The hidden curriculum of school grounds. http://files.eric.ed.gov/fulltext/ED430384.pdf (accessed 14 April 2003).

Tuan, Y.-F. (1977) *Space and Place. The Perspective of Experience*. Minneapolis and London: University of Minnesota Press.

Tuan, Y.-F. (1978) Children and the natural environment. In I. Altman and J.F. Wohlwill (eds) *Human Behaviour and Environment, Advances in Theory and Research. Vol. 3: Children and the Environment*. New York: Plenum Press, pp. 5–32.

Vasta, R. (ed.) (1992) *Six Theories of Child Development: Revised Formulations and Current Issues*. London: Jessica Kingsley.

Verbeek, P. and de Waal, B.M. (2002) The primate relationship with nature: biophilia as a general pattern. In P.H. Kahn and S.R. Kellert (eds) *Children and Nature. Psychological, Sociocultural and Evolutionary Investigations.* Cambridge, MA: MIT Press, pp. 1–28.

Wattchow, B. and Brown, M. (2011) *A Pedagogy of Place. Outdoor Education for a Changing World.* Clayton, Vic., Australia: Monash University.

CHAPTER 4

Awe and wonder

The elemental play model very much reflects the ecological systems model of Bronfenbrenner; each system or layer responds dynamically with each other, and when in harmony, the family, environment and service arrangements surrounding the child work in a reciprocal partnership, with any change at any time influencing the child's overall development. We recognise the terms 'micro', 'meso', 'macro' and 'exo systems' to, putting it simply, represent the child within the family, local community settings and cultures, and the values expressed through legislation and governance. The chrono system places the child within a socio-cultural and environmental time frame of more global concerns. Roszak (1998) confirms this idea: 'Every person's lifetime is anchored within a greater, universal lifetime. Each of us shares the whole of life's time on earth. Salt remnants of ancient oceans flow through our veins, ashes of expired stars rekindle in our genetic chemistry.'

In his foreword, Bronfenbrenner (1979: vii) cites Goethe, who commented: 'Everything has been thought of before, the difficulty is to think of it again.' What is being explored in this chapter is whether a spiritual system would help us 'think again' about a 'dimension to child development in addition to the physical, social, emotional and cognitive aspects' (Kimes Myers, 1997: xi). This 'thinking again', and scope of elemental play, provides an additional, spiritual system to Bronfenbrenner's model. Kimes Myers (ibid.) suggests that

> Although they [researchers and psychologists] are working to put their thoughts about spirituality and the young child into words, they are struggling to do so. Until there are ways to understand and name spiritual life within the secular world, a dynamic component of development will remain ignored. This severely limits our ability to address issues related to the 'whole child' – even as we claim that this is what we do.

This chapter explores how the concept of elemental play may help us put our thoughts about awe and wonder and spiritual development in young children into words, if you like, part of the unknown fascinating story of what we feel it is to be human. Chapter 5 will consider natural elements in detail, and whether all of our enjoyment of 'messing about' and 'being in our element' may have some deeper resonance with the natural world. For many cultures, this resonance forms a major part of belief systems and socio-cultural connections between humans and the places we inhabit.

Spiritual memory

Many authors have researched and written extensively about early and distinct memories of deeply spiritual experiences (Carson, 1956, 1962; Bateson, 1972; Robinson, 1977; E.O. Wilson, 1984; Coles, 1990; Roszak, 1991, 1995, 2002; Berleant, 1992; Chawla, 1994, 2002; Abraham, 1996; Kimes Myers, 1997; Erricker et al., 1997; Hay and Nye, 2006; Metzner, 1999; Wright, 2000; Hart, 2003; Eaude, 2006; Louv, 2005, 2012). They narrate the stories of children, indigenous cultures and young people who have encountered *something greater* than themselves when out in the wilderness, or when experiencing a majestic landscape. Many of the stories are the simpler memories of walking and *being in* familiar and outdoor places as a child. Some have been retold as religious experiences, with Hay and Nye (2006: 26) citing Robinson who 'noticed that a sizeable proportion of the 5000 or so accounts of religious experiences which had been sent to the unit were reminiscences of events occurring in childhood, sometimes in very early years.' Further, Robinson adds (1977: 41, 44):

> of all those approached [researched correspondents] nearly three quarters saw their childhood experiences as no more than the first steps in a process of growing awareness which was not to be complete until later, if then.
>
> [A]s one correspondent puts it, the childhood experiences are all there, in all their vividness and immediacy, at the level of consciousness at which they were originally experienced. And there they must wait, to be reactivated when the whole personality has reached a state of development at which this can take place. This may only be possible when 'I am ready to enter into certain experiences that will help to reactivate the earlier ones, thus making me consciously aware of them and of the link between what I experience now and what I experienced then as a child'. This is not nostalgia, it is a recovery of something lost, a reintegration into an ongoing life of something not treasured as a sentimental memory but found to have a new meaning.

Some stories have been recalled by adults when having mystic experiences in the wilderness. The memories are recalled as vivid and stable, that is, they have remained with the person over many years into adulthood and are easy to recall, although perhaps more difficult to explain to another person; the jewels (Chawla) and ark (Shepard) as recalled in the previous chapter. Many of us have been asked to think about an encounter or experience or scene from early childhood, one that fills us with a feeling of awe and beauty and I would perhaps defy anyone who is not able to *bring to mind* a place where they have been or can still be awed by the beauty or power of the natural world. Lake Wanaka, in the country of the long, white cloud (Aotearoa), the *ark* of elemental play was and is awesome, lifting the ideas and dialogue beyond any conversation I have shared.

Akin to mindfulness and underpinning the practice of hypnotherapy, this focus of being in the moment or *in one's element* is distinctly human; our species appears to be the only group capable of altering our perceptive sense: 'From one modern viewpoint, spirituality is rooted in something as concrete as breathing or eating or seeing; that is to say, it is biologically natural to the species *Homo Sapiens*' (Hay and Nye, 2006: 22).

For Carson (1956/1998: 15) and her nephew, early memories are stored when she carried him to the beach in rainy darkness:

> Out there, just at the edge of where we couldn't see, big waves were thundering in, dimly seen white shapes that boomed and shouted and threw great handfuls of froth at us. Together we laughed for pure joy – he a baby meeting for the first time the wild tumult of Oceanus. I with the salt of half a lifetime of sea love in me. But I think we felt the same spine-tingling response to the vast, roaring ocean and the wild night around us.

Her nephew was twenty months old, but I was reminded of this experience in 2015 with a baby of five months.

The physical feeling of his little body told me that he was in a heightened state of excitement; it was tense but responsive with my support being just that, a frame for him to lean against and stand upright. The urge to walk into the sea felt quite strong in him! He almost stopped breathing and this 'catching of the breath' can be something we all experience in times of great joy, wonder, fear, exhilaration and sadness – high levels of feeling, imagination and thinking when our sensory awareness is elevated.

ENCOUNTER: Elliot at the sea-edge

I walked him down to the sea, carrying him upright and looking forward so he could see where he was going and what he was walking towards. I was singing and slightly swaying. At the sea-edge, I crouched down and propped him on my thighs. At first he was very still but as I lifted him so that his little feet could touch the incoming waves, his body became a little more rigid and his arms began moving. As the waves receded, his feet lifted one by one as if he was trying to walk. His visual focus was on the sea, not on his feet or his hands, which slightly dipped as each small wave lapped in over his feet. From a crouch, I went to a sitting position (in order to maintain his standing position), his hands opening and shutting as each wave came in and went out. Feet gently paddling, Elliot and the sea; absorbed, alert and in his element.

Wonder

His experience, to me, was wonderful. Cobb (1977/1993: 28) agrees:

> Wonder is, first of all, a response to the novelty of experience (although not to be totally unexpected, which tends to arouse anxiety). Wonder is itself a kind of expectancy of fulfilment. The child's sense of wonder, displayed as surprise and joy, is aroused as a response to the mystery of some external stimulus that promises 'more to come' or better still, 'more to do' – the power of perceptual participation in the known and unknown.

Mills (n.d.) reiterates:

> My family and I were lucky enough to spend six weeks every summer in a glorified shed on the south coast of England. Mudeford Spit is a large strip of sand that separates the sea from the harbour, dotted with wooden huts. Life revolves around the rhythms of the sun, moon and tide. Children are free till they drop. I remember one night at the age of five lying deep in the cleavage of a sand dune. I shone a torch into the blue-black sky and immediately felt as small as the grains of sand I lay upon. I experienced a profound connection with the vast expanse of star-studded sky. The beam of light from my torch projected me into another world of possibilities. I remember thinking about infinity and wondering whether such a concept existed or not. That feeling of awe and wonder is still with me today.

Cobb (1977/1993: 88) argues that 'These vivid experiences, described retrospectively by adults, appear to be universal and suggest some universal link between mind and nature as yet uncodified but latent in consciousness in intuitive form'. Elemental play confirms this link. Sebba (cited in Wilson, 2007) concurs: children experience phenomena in a natural environment 'in a deep and direct manner, not as a background for events, but rather, as a factor and stimulator'. Elliot by the sea, Carson with her nephew near the ocean, Mills in a sand dune, my encounter under a swirling waterfall known as the 'washing machine' in Milton Sound, New Zealand, where I screamed breathlessly with joy and almost panic, are not everyday experiences for many of us. Vivid experiences, nevertheless, can be observed in playgrounds, woods, lush vegetation, gardens, fields and ditches and amongst stones and gravel, where children appear to revel in both the minute and the grand, especially within their own time frame. One can feel and see children experience an introspective silence.

One recalls Oliver, a three year old, a couple of years ago, starting forest school with some trepidation at leaving mum, and needing lots of time to approach the base we had created and the mud play in the puddles that had formed after heavy rain. By the end of the first session, he was wading and running and 'ploughing' (his word) through the mud. The following week after walking the perimeter a couple of times with me to recognise the woodland, he joined in with building a stick city in the remaining wet mud. On the third week, the puddle and mud had largely disappeared and some of the other children were digging to find the wet mud. Oliver, quietly watching, said 'If you dig all the world, there will be no world left.' For me this was profound and *big*; a big idea connecting a young child's thoughts with significant environmental insight, perhaps relating to ideas and images already assimilated but also a deep relationship over the past few weeks with lots of but then diminishing amounts of water and mud in the woods. Kimes Myers (1997: 21–2), like many of us early years practitioners, has watched, got involved with and encouraged mud play, and she asks us to

> Think with me about young children as they examine the physical properties of mud puddles. They step and stomp and splash in mucky water, dragging sticks through the damp sludge and tossing pebbles with anticipation of the coming plop as the small stones sink out of sight. We can only imagine what sense they are making of the experience. We understand that knowledge about the mud puddles and sinking stones is what we have come to call physical knowledge. What one's friends, and brothers and sisters and others do together and the way they interact in the process in mud puddle play is what we have come to call social knowledge. But how one feels about the mud puddle experience is personal knowledge. It is within the realm of personal knowledge that all other areas of knowledge become integrated, and it is within this realm that we can further examine 'spirit' and the related term 'spirituality'.

The role of imagination and spirituality

One of the main activities of this particular group of children was boundary walking. During the summer, nettles, grasses and cow parsley were taller than the children. The children walked, not seeing each other for quite a few paces, calling to each other, and then exclaiming when they emerged into the light; the tree canopy was also dark with large, summer leaves. They imagined monsters, hunters, footprints; the woodland *was* a forest and as Oliver's mum said to me: 'Being able to do forest school takes us back to using imagination.'

Using our imagination, Gussin Paley (1927/2004: 8) suggests 'provides the nourishing habitat for the growth of cognitive, narrative, and social connectivity in young children' and arguably 'the way we ascribe meaning to the deeper level of existence that surrounds us and is in us and our relationships' (Kimes Myers, 1997: 62). Robinson (1977) calls this 'original vision', with Webster (2002) helpfully suggesting

> 'spiritual' is derived from the Greek *pneumatikos*, and is closely related to the term 'inspiration' (*theopneustos*). The individual and community are understood to be *inspired or motivated* by spirit, which is understood to be that particular aspect which refers to their life principle – their inner vitality – with emotions and motivations.

Becker (1994: 257, cited in Kimes Myers, 1997: 19) simply states 'in its broadest definition, spirituality is "a code word for the depth dimension of human existence"'. Here, there seems to be a clear link with our understanding of well-being. Watching a 'vital' child enjoying a range of activities, with different children and adults, or contentedly playing alone with a variety of materials within a number of environments, we would say that their well-being is strong and assured. This high level of well-being (see Wardle and Vesty, 2015) affords the child the opportunity to create, problem solve, imagine, sustain friendships, follow through ideas and self-initiated projects, and assimilate new information; without this, all other aspects of development may be threatened. Early years practitioners would agree that a child's well-being is nurtured within the micro-system of loving carers and family within a supportive community. Kimes Myers (1997: 61–3) takes this further:

> The terms 'spirit' and 'spirituality' give us a way to talk about the dynamics of development – the spirit present within the children and an understanding of spirituality as that which surrounds and flows through the children, families, communities, and extended networks of caring others.
>
> A spirituality of caring is a way of naming what it is we do as a community to nurture and educate spirited young children for the invitations to transcendence presented by life; this is human activity performed by and for whole people in a whole community. Children are whole people and so are we. As Erikson (1964: 136) emphasizes, 'whole children need a whole world to be whole in.'

A spirituality of caring, then, can be described as the shared construct of those within a given

> community who support, nurture, guide, teach, and learn in caring, hopeful ways. There are four such core conditions in a spirituality of caring:
>
> - the provision of hospitable space;
> - the acceptance, embracing, and providing of experiences;
> - the presence of authentic, caring adults;
> - an affirmation of the process of learning . . . of being able to spiritedly transcend present conditions.
>
> (Myers and Myers, 1992, cited in Kimes Myers, 1997: 63)

This, Hardy (1965, cited by Hay and Nye, 2006: 22) argues 'is potentially present in all human beings and which has a positive function in enabling individuals to survive in their natural environment'.

Well-being seems enhanced by being outside. We feel better, more vital, energised and calmer. From personal forest school experiences, outdoor work and play, reading accounts and observations of others, the following comments will be familiar to you:

- He will just play for hours [Oliver's mum].
- Freedom to do things without worrying . . . working in a small group has really helped him. I think it has brought on his confidence [McKenzie's mum].
- I've heard his voice in the forest more [forest school leader].
- It's the psychological space [Megan's mum].
- We always go outside to play now [parent research, 2015].
- The world outside! There is so much of a focus how to be in a classroom or sat inside with an ipad or tv, phone, play-station etc. I remember being outside rain or shine having the best adventures all completely made up [parent research, 2015].
- Each child has found something unique to them. I would say they are often the quieter children who perhaps don't normally throw themselves into the mainstream play of nursery. But in their own, preferred environment, they really open up and chat lots! It's lovely [Little Muddy Boots leader].
- Finding tadpoles in the stream we visit and being able to paddle alongside them and return to look for them each week. Visiting a muddy puddle whilst heading out for the walk and still being there watching the children play an hour later. Experiencing the recent solar eclipse; a handful of parents stayed and we felt the woods go cold [forest school leader].

Friluftsliv

Paddling with tadpoles to experiencing a solar eclipse – the minutiae of the outdoor world and a much greater encounter in nature, both, however, made more meaningful by direct experience in the company of adults and within the time frames of the children. The sky going dark and the air going cold are mysterious

---

ENCOUNTER: Max

'I founded a snail. I'm making a bed.' He collects small wooden discs, lines them up by the side of the tree. He spends five to ten minutes lining them up and says he wants to make a bed for the snails and looks for sticks. He takes some time thinking about how long the sticks should be. These are again put in lengths with smaller ones on top.

'They need leaves on top to keep them warm.' He chooses brown, ground covering leaves. Snails are delicately placed on one of the discs and Max carefully covers the snails with leaf bedding, talking to himself continuously. Two other children approach the activity. He continues to pile on the leaves. Poppy continues to find snails – her engaging interest from last week. Max starts making more beds as she arrives.

for children, as is thunder and lightning, strong winds, stormy seas, shooting stars, rainbows, snowfall, fog and a full moon; 'awe-full' and mysterious to many adults, too. Watching a child staring at a full, low moon and trying to contemplate that everyone in the whole world looks at the same moon is as special as watching a child with snails.

Norwegians call this *friluftsliv*, 'To "experience" nature is to open oneself up for all its qualities and values' (Tordsson, 2007: 66). Hay and Nye (2006: 71) ask: 'Could it be the case that children's perceptions of mystery in situations where, from an adult perspective, there is a simple explanation arise from as profound an experience as those of the contemplative philosopher or the theologian?'

> Spirituality, in its full range, including religious awareness, is entirely natural. It grows out of a biological predisposition which can either be obscured or enhanced by culture. Spirituality is the bedrock on which rests the welfare not only of the individual but also of society, and indeed the health of our entire planetary environment. I am speaking of love of humanity, sensuous affinity for the landscapes and life-forms of our world, awe before the immensity of the universe in which we find ourselves, and awareness of an interfusing presence through all of these.
>
> (Ibid.: 141)

Eco-psychology

There remains a hesitancy about defining and using the concept of spirituality to explain possible human connections with the universe. Roszak (1998) uses the term 'eco-psychology', defining it as

> Eco-psychology is a new field that is developing in recognition that human health cannot be separated from the health of the whole and must include mutually enhancing relationships between humans and the non-human world. At its core, eco-psychology suggests that there is a synergistic relation between planetary and personal well-being; that the needs of the one are relevant to the other . . . repression of the ecological unconscious is the deepest route of collusive madness in industrial society.
>
> For eco-psychology as for other therapies, the crucial stage of development is the life of the child. The ecological unconscious is regenerated as if it were a gift, in the newborn's enchanted sense of the world. Wordsworth's hymns to the child's love of nature are basic texts for developmental eco-psychology, a first step toward creating the ecological ego.

Taylor (2013) argues that this current psychological ideology emanates from the Romantic tradition of expressing powerful emotions springing from natural encounters, privileged through the poetry of Wordsworth and Taylor Coleridge, the theosophy of Rousseau and Steiner, and latterly the transcendentalist movement (Roszak, Metzner) in North America which has 'birthed' eco-psychology. It can make us all wistful and nostalgic for a 'natural and golden childhood', and that children and adults are now experiencing what Louv (2005) would call a 'nature deficit principle'. When contesting current wistful attitudes, Taylor (2013: 16) cites Philo (1992), who suggests 'the simple fact that things turn out differently in different places'. She also discusses the core principles espoused by Carson (1956/1998), Cobb (1977/1993) and, more recently, Chawla (2002):

> all of these nature education advocates share the same Romantic belief, passed on from Rousseau, and reiterated by Wordsworth and Thoreau amongst others, that children have an intrinsically special relationship with nature. From this basic premise, they all passionately advocate (like Rousseau) that the best kind of learning comes from children's direct, rather than mediated, nature experiences.
>
> (Taylor, 2013: 52)

Later in her challenging line of thought, what Taylor finally seems to be stating is

> we cannot locate human experience outside of nature and for this reason the social and the natural are best thought about together – as an imbroglio of human and nonhuman, living and inert, geographic and engineered, discursive and material relations.
>
> (Ibid.: 70)

The 'imbroglio' she describes, I would suggest, is similar to Kimes Myers' (1997: 109) 'inexhaustible web of meaning interrelatedly connecting self, other, world, and cosmos' and the elemental layer of the ecological systems model. It is more than nostalgia for any idyllic childhood; nor is it simply a reflection of the pedagogic traditions of Froebel, Rousseau, Pestalozzi, Steiner, Owens, McMillan, Dewey and Isaacs. They certainly put their philosophies to work in the outdoor environments created for young children, and yes, many were in response to growing industrialisation and moves away from agricultural communities. There seems to be something deeper, however, in their commitment to natural play experiences based on observing children's explorations and the well-being they recognised from elemental connections.

There are cultural and pedagogical traces of these philosophical beliefs and values in current early years practice, the majority without the religious convictions of Rousseau and Steiner, nevertheless, the elemental play hypothesis suggests that we have, to a greater or lesser extent, harmonious, ecological respect for the land, environment and spaces we co-habit with non-human species upon which we are dependent and connected. Our outdoor provision and approaches encourage children to respect and nurture the environment in which they play, from shrubs, to plant life, leaving insects under logs and spaces as we find them. This has been within the nature of caring humans from the beginning and passed through generations through encounters, narratives and exploratory behaviours.

Some thirty years ago, 'James Lovelock expounded the Gaia hypothesis that considers the biosphere to be a self-regulating system sensitive to the principle of life' (Moore and Cosco, 2003). This hypothesis is described in many different ways and within many cultures:

> John Rangihau, an elder of the *Tuhoe* tribe, has said that everything possesses a *mauri* (lifeforce) and that the Maori were very much aware of the environment and how much they owed to it. He believed, as do all Maori people, that there is an emotional tie to the land because of the way Maori people have been taught about their origins and about the whole myth of creation.
>
> (*Taounga Maori*, 2002: 40)

Maori epistemology has influenced the early education curriculum, Te Whāriki (Ministry of Education, 1996), and pedagogical practices in New Zealand. 'Te Whāriki is designed to be empowering, holistic, community-based, and fundamentally about reciprocal relationships with "people, places and things".'
(Carr and Rameka, 2005: 7, cited in Meade, n.d.)

Te Whāriki is compatible with both Maori beliefs and Bronfenbrenner's ecological theory of human development. Reedy (2003: 68–70) further explains the principle of Mana Atua:

> This is the development of personal well-being in the child, through an understanding of their own uniqueness and divine 'specialness'. According to Maori there is a divine spirit, a spark of godliness, in each child born into this world. This belief is rooted in the teachings of old. [. . .] The Maori mind also determined that all things, both animate and inanimate, have their own mauri, their own spark of godliness. Mana Aotāroa is the development of a desire to explore and understand all aspects of this world and the universe; the development of curiosity, and of seeking answers. The development of a child's mana is nurtured in the knowledge that they are loved and respected; that their physical, mental, spiritual, and emotional strength will build mana, influence, and control; that having mana is the enabling and empowering tool to controlling their own destiny.

Kimes Myers (1997: 87) recalls the narrative of Black Elk of the Oglala Sioux:

> The first peace, which is the most important, is that which comes within the souls of men when they realize their relationship, their oneness, with the universe and all its Powers, and when they realize that at the centre of the Universe dwells Wakan-Tanka and that this centre is really everywhere, it is within each of us.

Tuan (1978: 22) talks of the Wogeo children in New Guinea and Tallensi children in northern Ghana who are thoroughly *at home* with both the ecological and spiritual environments of their clan settlements. Louv (2012: 246) cites (Berry, 1999) who claims:

> If we don't have certain outer experiences, we don't have certain inner experiences, or at least, we don't have them in a profound way. We need the sun, the moon, the stars, the rivers and the mountains and birds, the fish in the sea, to evoke a world of mystery, to evoke the sacred. It gives us a sense of awe.

When children are very young, it is the adults and more knowledgeable others who welcome them into experiences of the world around them; this may be an everyday encounter when walking under trees, following ladybirds, feeling sand and mud; it may be on a beach. Kimes Myers' (1997) 'spirituality of caring' reminds us of Rogoff's (2008: 63) 'guided participation' which

> includes deliberate attempts to instruct and incidental comments or actions that are overheard or seen as well as involvement with particular materials and experiences that are available, which indicate the direction in which people are encouraged to go or discouraged from going.

This reciprocal involvement can include the sharing of 'wonder-full' experiences, joint adventures and discoveries, dressing and acting appropriately in a range of environmental conditions, with a range of resources and materials, and the passing on of knowledge, stories and mysteries about the planet. Kellert (2002: 127) argue that 'Delight, elation, and affective engagement appear to form a crucible in which the child and later adult shape and mould an inclination for creativity and discovery.'

As Taylor (2013) has said, these seem to naturally occur within the different contexts, time and systems that encircle the child. We might also assume that the thoughts and perceptions of young children will stay unsaid, but not necessarily unfelt:

> For some children, experience of awe and wonder may begin at an early age and provide a defining orientation that becomes a long-term life focus. In a report to me, a woman (Joyce) claimed a childhood experience, at the age of three, in which her seven-year-old brother 'invited' her to 'see a surprise' that shaped her life-long understanding of the world. At midnight he woke her and showed her
>
>> *the full moon low in the southern sky. I have never seen the moon, did not really know it exists – now I am astonished by its utter beauty and glittering light. My brother tells me that the moon is a big ball out in space, just as the sun is . . . he tells me that we are on the world, called the earth, and that Earth is also a big ball*

> in the sky. I remember this, with wonder, all my life. So beautiful, these balls. I feel connected with these three balls: this is a feeling inside me. I don't speak of this to my parents, it is my own story (and picture), shared in some way with my brother. (Vancouver, BC, 1999)
>
> (Scott, 2004: 186–7)

One does not have to belong to or follow a particular religious convention to explore and sense a feeling of 'otherness'. Children's curiosity, questioning and inquiries about the natural events of life, death and the universe are suggestive of a spiritual quest in their identity development, demanding an answer to 'How do I belong to this big world?' Moments of total absorption in play suggest deep, inner involvement of the child; could this be spiritual contentment? In the next chapter, long-held beliefs about elemental connections are explored which amplify a spiritual and magical dimension to human evolution.

Provocations

- When did you last see a child express awe and wonder? How did you know?
- How might 'awe-full' and 'wonder-full' experiences create a zone of potential and empowering development, moving from the known to the unknown and vice versa?
- Recall 'big' questions children have asked and consider how you sustain their conversations and reflections. How *do* you answer and give space to their ideas?
- What do we mean when we say 'she is in her element'?
- To what extent are the young children in your care given opportunities to explore the natural environment and afforded time to develop into reflective, spiritual and kind members of the learning community?
- How far can we suggest that young children's absorbing interests are spiritual/innate and thus maturing human qualities?

References

Bronfenbrenner, U. (1979) *The Ecology of Human Development. Experiments by Nature and Design.* Cambridge, MA: Harvard University Press.

Carson, R. (1956/1998) *The Sense of Wonder.* New York: Harper Collins.

Cobb, E. (1977/1993) *The Ecology of Imagination in Childhood.* Putnam, CT: Spring Publications.

Gussin Paley, V. (1927/2004) *A Child's Work: The Importance of Fantasy Play.* Chicago: University of Chicago Press.

Hay, D. with Nye, R. (2006) *The Spirit of the Child*, rev. edn. London: Jessica Kingsley.

Kellert, S.R. (2002) Experiencing nature: affective, cognitive, and evaluative development in children. In P.H. Kahn, Jr. and S.R. Kellert (eds) *Children and Nature. Psychological, Sociocultural and Evolutionary Investigations*. Cambridge, MA: MIT Press, pp. 117–52.

Kimes Myers, B. (1997) *Young Children and Spirituality*. London: Routledge.

Louv, R. (2005) *Last Child in the Woods. Saving Our Children from Nature-Deficit Disorder*. Chapel Hill, NC: Algonquin.

Louv, R. (2012) *The Nature Principle. Reconnecting with Life in a Virtual Age*. Chapel Hill, NC: Algonquin.

Meade, A. (n.d.) Linking children to the land and the past. Unpublished paper, Wellington, New Zealand.

Mills, J. (n.d.) Children's relationships with outdoor spaces. Unpublished.

Ministry of Education (1996) *Te Whāriki*. Wellington, NZ: Learning Media.

Moore, R.C. and Cosco, N.G. (2003) Developing an earth-bound culture through design of childhood habitats. www.naturallearning.org/earthboundpaper.html (accessed 19 March 2006).

Reedy, T. (2003) Toku Rangatiratanga Na Te Mana-Mātauranga [Knowledge and power set me free]. In J. Nuttall (ed.) *Weaving Te Whāriki. Aotearoa New Zealand's Early Childhood Curriculum Document in Theory and Practice*. Wellington, NZ: New Zealand Council for Educational Research.

Robinson, E. (1977) *A Study of the Religious Experience of Childhood*. Oxford: Religious Education Centre.

Rogoff, B. (2008) Observing sociocultural activity on three planes. In K. Hall, P. Murphy and J. Soler (eds) *Pedagogy and Practice: Culture and Identities*. Milton Keynes: Open University Press, pp. 58–74.

Roszak, T. (1998) Ecopsychology: eight principles. www.taichisage.com/content/ecopsych8.htm (accessed 1 July 2016).

Scott, D. (2004) Spirituality and children: paying attention to experience. In H. Goelman et al. (eds) *Multiple Lenses Multiple Images: Perspectives on the Child across Time, Space, and Disciplines*. Toronto: University of Toronto Press.

Taonga Maori: A Spiritual Journey Expressed Through Maori Art. (2002) National Museum Guide. Wellington, NZ: Te Papa Press.

Taylor, A. (2013) *Reconfiguring the Natures of Childhood*. London: Routledge.

Tordsson, B. (2007) What is friluftsliv good for? Norwegian friluftsliv in a historical perspective. In B. Henderson and N. Vikander (eds) *Nature First. Outdoor Life the Friluftsliv Way*. Canada: Natural Heritage Books.

Tuan, Y.-F. (1978) Children and the natural environment. In I. Altman and J.F. Wohlwill (eds) *Human Behaviour and Environment, Advances in Theory and Research. Vol. 3: Children and the Environment*. New York: Plenum Press, pp. 5–32.

Wardle, L. and Vesty, S. (2015) Exploring children's well-being and motivations. In A. Woods (ed.) *The Characteristics of Effective Learning: Creating and Capturing the Possibilities in the Early Years*. London: David Fulton.

Webster, S. (2002) *Spirituality: Providing Guidance through Uncertainty*. Clayton, Vic., Australia: Monash University. www.aare.edu.au/02pap/web02088.htm (accessed 2 August 2006).

Wilson, R.A. (2007) *The Wonders of Nature: Honoring Children's Ways of Knowing*. www.earlychildhoodnews.com/earlychildhood/article (accessed 27 July 2012).

CHAPTER

5

Being in one's element

> **CONVERSATION: Debbie Ryder**
>
> As I think about what I mean by elemental play, I initially think back to my first memories of when I was a very young child. It's strange, but most of what I can remember from being a very young child tends to be outside memories, either being outside with my mum as she hangs the clothes on the line, as she says to me 'look up – what can you see?', or sitting in the frothing tide outside my grandmother's house as it laps up around me, or walking through the fruit orchard on our farm and looking up through the tall trees. I'll always remember a tiny lake (more like a puddle than a lake really) that we had on our farm that my father named after me because I loved going there so much. Why is it that my most treasured memories are when I was so young? What must I have been feeling as a young child that cemented these experiences in my mind? What influences might these early fond experiences have had on the way I view the world now? Gebser (1985, cited in Chawla, 2002: 212) talks about an *archaic consciousness* that animals and young infants use called *arche*-Greek for 'origin'. This early conscious experience with nature that the infant has lasts for the period of infancy and then seems to go to the background of the child's life as she/he grows older; however, we may re-enter this experience later in life when as adults we feel a sense of being 'simply absorbed in our body, in our place'.

When absorbed and able to determine the place and time to think, especially when closely connected to the beach, the sand, the sea, the grass, the rocks and the mountains, my clarity of thought and senses seem to be elevated. It becomes clearer that a child could be in the same state of higher-level thinking, feeling and imagination *when in their element*. What do we understand by the phrase 'she is in her element'? She is at one, at ease, in control and emotionally satisfied. A working hypothesis of elemental play might be children exploring the 'I am', 'I can' and 'should I' through ideas and notions and inquiries which is the elemental process of finding out about self in relation to people, places and things through their discovery of the natural environment; in other words, playing. Csíkszentmihályi (1979, cited in Laevers, 2006: 24) speaks of 'the state of flow', 'an openness to (relevant) stimuli and the perceptual and cognitive functioning has an intensity which is lacking in other kinds of activity'. The intensity of feeling or oneness and belonging lead to high levels of involvement with one's ideas and activities, and also to a deep sense of well-being. Elemental playfulness could be an instinctive, human and cultural disposition and using this possible lens gives us a phenomenological tool to interpreting behaviour. This behaviour suggests that a child is drawn to and demonstrates a deep sense of well-being when playing in a natural context, when engaging in elemental play. It suggests that very young children's interests are quite deeply spiritual and innate and observable; in other words, maturing human qualities.

Natural elements

We often observe children playing and being excited by natural materials – playing with earth, wood, stone and sand, and content to dig, scrape, taste, fill, pile and gauge. The child's action could be interpreted as mastering the natural elements surrounding them and feeling comfortable and at one with them: having a sense of well-being and belonging and a sense of 'I am'. Children appear to be content for longer when handling natural materials. This is more extensive than calling it 'heuristic' play or exploratory play. It seems to be more elemental than that. It is more than play with natural objects; it is also about the environmental and spiritual use and respect of elements.

If we recognise and recall this affinity with natural objects and elements, we are helping children with their sensori-motor, emotional, social, physical and cognitive development and building on their very early explorations. It is possible that we are maintaining spiritual and cultural links with what has gone before.

Playing with and exploring the elements appears to have a cultural, spiritual and genetic fingerprint, furthermore, natural elements – earth, air, water and fire – hold a fundamental fascination for very young children right up to adulthood as we try to recall their wonder and re-create or master their power and potential. Anthropologically, humans have evolved due to their exploration, dexterity, imagination, problem solving and community activities and what we see very young children doing is reflecting early human development and biophilia – an 'innate, hereditary emotional attraction to nature and other living organisms' (White and Stoeklin, 1998). White (2014: 48) concurs: 'Young children are endlessly interested in and biologically programmed to explore the stuff of the earth, how materials behave and what they do.' From this perspective, it may be possible to imagine how the elemental affordance of earth, wind, water and fire could form

> **CONVERSATION: Debbie Ryder**
>
> The *very early* experiences of an infant of *rock*, *earth*, *water*, *light*, *leaf* and *love* from the original *elements* lead to the identity of early 'conscious' thought and needs. The infant must know that they are 'safe' and also free to experience these fundamental 'joys' of being an infant. The infant is establishing a clear 'sense of self' as she has been able to experience the elements of nature for herself. The elements of the natural world are not interpreted by her caregiver as a threat to her safety; in fact, they are viewed as *elements of learning*.
>
> *Fond memories* are then attached to these learning experiences and these are then 'stowed away', and as she is about to approach a new time in her life, she will not be calling on these *original elements of learning* very often and will, instead, seek other challenges to assist her learning. But these original elements never quite leave her; instead, they 'guide' her in an *intuitive*, unconscious manner as she seeks to form relationships with those who are close to her, and places that are important to her. The depth of those early, original elemental learning experiences that occurred will determine the depth of instinct that will see her through these life experiences.
>
> That will be when she calls up her *fond memories*, and *instinct* and *intrigue* will once again unite her with *rock*, *earth*, *water*, *light*, *leaf* and *love*, and she will experience joy and feel a sense of coming together of self and other, absorbed in body and place.

a crucial link between early childhood learning and development, and the continued survival and evolution of the human species.

Four elements

In Chapter 8, I will consider Nicholson's (1971) 'loose parts theory' in more detail, but the four natural elements above seem to be the malleable and fascinating 'stuff' that children are so keen to explore from their very first encounters with the natural world. The four elements have a long history of cultural significance from Ancient Greek philosophy to medieval physic, and weave through many religions such as Buddhism. For many indigenous people, the significance remains both mystic and 'awe-full'. In some ideologies, the number of elements increases. For example:

> Buddhist thought divides the universe into two categories: the physical universe, which is thought of as a receptacle or 'container' (*bhajana*), and the 'beings' (*sattva*) or life-forms which reside in it. The physical universe is formed by the interaction of the five elements, namely earth, water, fire, air and space. Through the interaction of the five elements there evolve 'world-systems'. These world-systems are thought to undergo cycles of evolution and decline lasting billions of years. Naturally, the beings who inhabit the physical

universes are not unaffected by these events, and indeed there is some suggestion that it is the moral status of the inhabitants that determine the fate of the world-system.

(Keown, 1996: 30)

Rupp (2005: 12, 48–9) offers further analysis:

> So what did the Greeks mean by 'element'? The terms translated as 'matter', 'substance', 'attribute' and 'element' were all introduced into philosophy in the 4th century. Empedocles refers to them as *rhizomata* – roots. The Greek concept of a small number of basic elements that comprise all matter is found in cultures around the globe. The ancient Chinese postulated a cosmos based on 5 elements – fire, water, earth, wood and metal. The Indians originally hypothesised three – fire, water and earth, later expanded to include air and the nebulous ether, or void.
>
> Earth, air, fire and water are still said to shape our psyches. Most of all, however, the 4 elements continue to exert their power because it's through them that we first and best experience the world. In a way, as each of us strives to make sense of the complex reality that surrounds us, we retrace the path that the Greeks took. All of us begin at that beginning, and build upon what we discover there. Our initial experience of the elements opens before us the rich diversity of the physical world.

Rupp (ibid.) also explores Galen's theory of personality where elements were seen to determine behaviour until well into the seventeenth century and considered by Jung as the basis of four personality functions during the 1920s. Metzner (1999: 29, 32–3) considers medieval philosophy as reflecting

> a worldview in which human nature is perceived as embedded or nested within the larger world of nature . . . and is now gaining favour in living systems theory, which describes a world of complex, patterned interrelationships at many levels of reality.
>
> [Of the many traditional person/planet myths and analogies] the individual human organism-person is viewed as the created vehicle or form of an immortal spirit or divine being – and so is earth.

Elemental play draws on understandings that infant development is also 'embedded or nested within the larger world of nature'. Moore and Cosco (2003) also write about Lovelock's Gaia hypothesis 'that considers the biosphere to be a self-regulating system sensitive to the principle of life'; underlining

> The biological health of the planet and the health of the world's children are interdependent. Together they form a single ecosystem under the potential influence and protection of the social construct of sustainable development. Childhood is the most critical stage in the human life cycle. A small but growing

TABLE 5.1 Metzner's organic correspondences

	INDIVIDUAL	PLANET
Earth	bones, muscles, flesh, tissues	soil, minerals, rock, vegetation
Air	breath, respiration, sound, voice	winds, atmosphere, clouds
Water	blood, lymph, humours, hormones	oceans, tides, lakes, rain, rivers
Fire	brain, nerves, subtle energies	lightning, bioelectricity, radiation

body of research indicates that daily experience of nature, spending time outdoors in the fresh air and sunlight, in touch with plants and animals, has a measurable impact on healthy child development.

There appears to be a possible connection here to the idea of an elemental 'layer' as part of Bronfenbrenner's ecological systems theory and how different cultures, at different times and in different contexts are rhizomatic; each culture or rhizome finding its roots or a way to explain natural order and the properties of the world around them. Metzner (1999: 32–3) goes further, making connections between the body and planetary constituents.

Water

Having pondered and hypothesised about elemental play for some years and discussed ideas with students and colleagues, it seems possible to use this lens to investigate the actions of very young children as *another way of looking*, or 're-envisaging the actions of very young children from an innate and ecological developmental perspective' (Ryder, pers. comm., 2016). Those of us committed to outdoor play will have no doubt of the value, creativity, involvement and imagination afforded by natural materials, changing seasons and the changes observed when elements combine together naturally or through the actions of adults and children. The experiences are scientific, sensory and magical, and have geographic and historical significance; they are also messy, fun and unpredictable, 'a riot of distinctive and unique organisms that move, grow, reproduce, and often seemingly feel and think' (Carson, 1956/1998: 140).

We see young children drawn to water – and all liquids – as they experience flow, cause and effect. Water is an element with pre-natal memories and early tactile and affective satisfaction. There are few babies who dislike their first warm early baths in sinks, or baby baths or skin-to-skin in a big bath with a parent, and when older, to drip and pour water from a feeding cup to watch a small puddle form. As a young child in Reggio Emilia observed in documentation (1996, 'The sea is born from the mother wave'): 'I was all wet, I was in water inside a balloon ... I didn't ask them if I had a bathing suit on.' Water is estimated to make up 78 per cent of our bodies as babies, decreasing to 65 per cent as adults (Utz, n.d.), so it is not surprising that children feel and can be observed as having a close affinity with water and all that playing with water can offer. Your list would be similar to mine: filling, flowing, dripping, mixing with other materials, swimming, splashing, freezing, melting, floating on, sailed over, dammed up – all active *and* significant to exploratory and expeditionary behaviour demonstrated by generations of surviving and developmental species. Nomadic hunter-gatherers evolved into farming communities because of cultivating habits and cultivation depended on harnessing the power and properties of water, which covers 71 per cent of the earth's surface.

Malaguzzi (1996: 80) wrote:

> *The city in the rain* is one of the infinite 'versions' of the city, linked to particular events that shift the children's experiences, perceptions, and thoughts. The city becomes part of a double stage-set that is as unexpected as it is spectacular. The streets, objects, monuments, and lampposts are still there, strong and unmoving, but here they give way to the *protagonism* [my italics] of the rain: thunder, lightning, dark storm clouds, noises, smells, changes of colour, the sparkling of asphalt, water streaming down the streets, puddles, and most of all people who improvise and adapt their behavior, pulling out umbrellas and rain-hats, running zig-zag for cover, making stops that change the course of conversations and feelings.

The children's explanations are inspiring:

> The water comes down from the sky, its rain, and it goes down the mountain, goes into the holes in the mountain, and goes down into the lake that's there at the bottom of the mountain. Then there's a canal that slopes down that carries the water first to a lake and then to the aqueduct. There are lots of passages under the ground, and the mice drink some of the water. They just drink a little, and the rest goes onto the fountains. It goes up the rocks of the fountain . . . then the rock is like a slide and the water goes back down.
>
> (Elisa)

Some of you may have seen the Reggio Emilia documentary 'The Amusement Park for Birds' (*Il luna park degli uccellini*) and marvelled and the development of the project where children think about, research, design and execute a series of constructions for the birds to enjoy.

> For days on end, the children will play and work with the water, the taps, pipes, sluice gates, sprays, tanks, basins, canals, water wheels, reservoirs, and the relationship between the inclination of the channels and the speed of the water.
>
> (Reggio Children, 1995: 72)

When asking parents at Little Muddy Boots what their children most enjoyed during their play sessions, their replies reflected observations made over many years:

- Free play with water. Erin goes straight for the water every week!
- Mud pies and water play.
- Going off site to do the pond dipping.
- Muddy play [the water butt is adjacent to the mud kitchen].
- Trip to the pond.
- Exploring water and how it flows. The girls love the watering cans and watching each other fill up the bottles. [There is a pipe and funnel system attached to a fence a few metres from the water butt.]
- Watering plants.
- Mud kitchen and watering activities which he returns to most weeks.

Hannah (leader of Little Muddy Boots) has commented that parents have now talked about creating their own mud kitchen or water wall in their own gardens. A parent also commented 'Come rain or shine we are out there! I love that a rainy day doesn't mean a bored Marie day! Come rain or shine you can play outside!'

Laevers (cited in May et al., 2006: 13) describes children learning effectively as looking like 'fish in water'; we may interpret this as being in one's element. Observing young children learning effectively, using the Leuven scales (Laevers, 1994), generally results in a high level of involvement score.

Playing with and learning about water make up the focus of the majority of observations I have made of children outside and this may be because I feel particularly comfortable or in my element with water and because children seem to gravitate towards water activity outside. Water play is generally more restricted inside. The Reggio projects have inspired many preschools, children's centres and

---

ENCOUNTER: At preschool: assessing levels of involvement

Felicity had focused on a spontaneous play opportunity outside where large templates and chalks were placed near the exit door. A child had asked for water to be able to brush through the template and this had become a busy, involved activity. Adult 2, Felicity and I discussed this activity because of the high levels of involvement (5) and enjoyment. I asked A2 why she thought the activity might have been so engaging. Her response was that it was new. I suggested the messiness, open-ended and risky nature of the activity (risky as in spontaneous, child-led process rather than product) and we discussed how the activity could be extended and re-sited away from the door to a larger area with more water, larger brushes, chalks, paint and pebbles.

Source: Woods (2016: 35)

Being in one's element

> **ENCOUNTER: Collecting rain**
>
> 1. The woodland was soggy. It seemed to have rained for weeks. The heavy canopy of leaves created a dark and gloomy play space and we quickly erected roof tarpaulins between trees. The children wore fluorescent jackets and head torches and were excited to run in and out of the shelter. Tom, one of the tallest, jumped and tipped some of the collecting water *accidentally* off the edge of the roof, then wanted to repeat this; we thought about how long it might take to collect a sufficient amount of water to pour off the top. (As adults, our roof design was flawed – a puddle was collecting in the middle of the roof, not running off a sloped roof.) Tom watched the water collecting in a puddle for a while, then ran off to fetch a long bough and asked for help to stand it in the middle of the den to create a 'pitched roof'. (His explanation.) We did this together, and water was now running off in two or three places. He said that we could collect it and went and found the bottles which were already full of drinking water; he tipped them out to collect 'real water'. Over the next 15–20 minutes, Tom compared how quickly the bottles filled off a pitched roof and with the bough taken away, from the rain puddle tipped from the roof. He seemed satisfied with his goal, preferred the cascade rather than the gradual flow and could explain flow, pitch, depth, speed.
> 2. At the edge of the verandah outside the classroom, the guttering and down pipes from the flat roof let rain water flow down a small grate; occasionally, the flow of water was too great and afforded puddle play. Mohammed was a child with an apparent vertical and connecting schema, always building, constructing, joining resources together and he began to watch the water flow from the down pipe, showing concern that the playground would become flooded. He collected a bucket from the sandpit and held it underneath the pipe, collected the rain, took it to another drain, tipped it out, returned and repeated this activity for some time before asking us if we had any more pipes. An idea had seemed to come to him to extend the pipework to 'carry the water' away from the small drain, to the one he had been using to tip his own bucket. The next day it was not raining but he asked for the crates, pipes and guttering to build a drainage and outflow system with water collected from the tap. Mohammed was investigating flow, drainage, volume and work efficiency.
>
> *Source*: Woods (2015: 98)

nurseries to design water courses and watery opportunities in their outdoor play environments and most young children have access to at least a water tray indoors. It is a very relaxing medium, where thoughts and ideas are *in flow*.

The two children here are considering the properties of water and how to manage it scientifically. Water also appears to be helpful when children are feeling less assured, as seen with Oliver in Chapter 2 and with Amy below.

> **ENCOUNTER: Amy and the seaweed**
>
> At twenty months, Amy was experiencing her first beach and I watched as her mum took her down to the waves and the hard, wet sand. Amy looked pretty scared; the large expanse of noisy waves and the gritty, hard and wet sand was not to her liking. She did not want to be put down and pointed back to the dry sand closer to the top of the beach. Her mum was disappointed and I suggested that the next day, we try some activities that would help her enjoy the beach environment more. The next day, after some play in the dry sand, I said to them both, 'shall we go and get some water in the bucket?' There was a shallow pool by the side of a groyne and I walked ahead to fill the bucket, pouring the water back into the pool while she walked down. A few buckets pouring from me, and she took the bucket to do this for herself. Her actions were repetitive: fill, sit down, pour water from the near side of the bucket, down her tummy, wait and fill the bucket again, and again and again . . . The groyne had lots of hanging seaweed and I pulled some off, placing it into her empty bucket; this became a new activity. It was hard to pull away from the wood; she used lots of strength and masses of concentration. Pull, sit, fill; pull, sit fill. I should think about forty-five minutes had passed. I suggested to her mum that we wait until she was ready to finish before going back up to the dry sand. We knew when it was *her time* to end the play. She sat down, looked up at us and held her arms out to be carried, back to get dry and warm and ready for tea.
>
> *Source*: Moran and Brown (2013: 87)

Earth

White (n.d.) further explores the well-being of children in her textual introduction to 'Making a Mud Kitchen':

> There is little more important in our physical world than earth and water and they are truly intriguing things, especially when they interact. Mixing soil, water and a range of other materials has a foundational role in early childhood which has deep importance and endless possibilities for well-being, development and learning.

Rupp (2005: 19) considers the four element model as

> to arrange themselves in concentric layers, with elemental earth positioned solidly at the centre, water wrapped around it, air encircling water, and fire – the most volatile of the 4, the last before the heavenly ether. As an extra wrinkle, each element was imbued with associated qualities of hot, cold, wet, or dry; and it was postulated that interchanges among these qualities allowed

one element to transmogrify into another. Air, being hot and wet, could be cooled, thereby converting it to water, which was cold and wet; water, in turn could be dried, converting it to cold, dry earth.

And at the very centre of this model sits the child. There are very few children who do not enjoy the luxurious messiness of mud, sand, or clay with or without water, or a glorious mixture of each. It crumbles, oozes, liquefies, makes solids and can be used as paste and as building material; children model it, imagine with it and find that it can hold its shape.

During Tom's rain-catching encounter above, three children used the cups of water for their own activity.

To deconstruct this encounter would be to deny the holistic nature of the playful learning observed and as readers you will see the value of it as experienced by the children. Steiner is reflected in Faarlund's (2007: 56–7) observation:

> For ages, the lifestyles of humankind were inspired by a 'touch the Earth' philosophy. The natural rhythms of the plants – seasons, diurnal rhythms and growth rhythms – were not gravely abused until the onset of the industrial revolution. Thus, humankind grew up on a planet with free natural rhythms, which obviously left deeply rooted patterns in us.

There was rhythm in the children's movement as well as rhythm in the chanting which evolved through joyful play and messiness. Children digging, building with sand and stones, scooping tunnels and pounding clay are physical activities; they generally involve ready-made or improvised tools, the constructions often mimicking more ancient builds that they cannot have experienced, and repeated through generations of evolving and successful builders.

Rupp (2005: 317) suggests: 'Of the species of modern man, the earliest, *Homo habilis*, is named for his/her inventive cleverness with stones: *habilis* means toolmaker.' Time and time again I have seen children collecting, transporting, hoarding, building with, feeling them flow through their hands, and throwing stones into water. There is empowerment and desire here, for 'Earth is the first element of science and technology, art and architecture, and the military-industrial complex. Our first tools were stones' (ibid.: 316).

Chawla (2006: 68) concurs:

> What [children] find in the natural world rewards their initiatives and encourages their continuing engagement. Children see immediate, reinforcing effects of their actions, which simultaneously show them how the world works and their own capabilities. The wet earth keeps the shape they press it into – unless they add too much water and it turns to runny mud. That means try it again with less water next time. That leads to the next time . . . and when the earth moulds just right, nearby stones and grasses make perfect decorative touches.

> **ENCOUNTER: Mud-paint**
>
> Anthony: You are in charge Evie, keep on walking. We can both be in charge.
>
> Megan, Anthony and Evie walk straight to the 'sticky mud'!
>
> Megan: Look at my footprint!
> Evie: I think it's ice cream for the trees. *(A bucket of mud)*
> Anthony: How many cups are there?
>
> Evie counts one to nine.
>
> Anthony: How many people are there today?
> Evie: Nine.
> Anthony: We're making it look slippy aren't we?
>
> The trio spend twenty minutes painting the trees, with Megan smoothing mud onto the tree in a very fluid motion. Erin joins them and uses a paintbrush, not getting her hands in the mud. Anthony and Evie sing:
>
>> 'Muck, muck on the tree everywhere, mucky, mucky, mucky, muck, muck, muck' *(it is quite rhythmic)*
>> 'Monkey, monkey, monkey' *(six times repeat)*
>> 'Everywhere, everywhere' *(four times repeat)*
>> 'Mucky shoes, mucky shoes' *(four times repeat)*
>
> Anthony: Make this all soft now I've got some more for this branch.
>
>> 'Muckiest week. Marky, marky, marky!'
>
> Anthony: We're making the branch look silly . . . I'm standing up on my tiptoes.
> Evie: Here are mucky, here are mucky everywhere.
>
> Anthony and Evie walk away from the tree to collect sticks to stick on the tree on top of the mud.
>
> At recall time, Megan said she enjoyed getting muddy: 'I used the tub. I put my hands in and squeezed it.' Erin said, 'I used the paint *(pause)* the tree with a paint brush with dirt.'

Children's interest in working with water and earth reflects not only the messiness of creative and sensory exploration but also the most significant elements of survival and human evolution. White (2014: 48) suggests 'Young children are endlessly interested in and biologically programmed to explore the stuff of the earth, how materials behave and what they do (Kellert 1993) . . . the central role of earth and water in the workings of the world'.

Fire

Children are also drawn, when permitted, to light and heat: fire, lights, sparks, the contrast of light and dark. Projects in Reggio Emilia often reflect this observed interest. These are all natural forces/elements. We feel an emotional resonance to movement, light and space. It has also 'been a vehicle of worship, supernatural appeasement, and spiritual communion' (Rupp, 2005: 221).

Light is considered a guiding teaching strategy in Reggio-inspired learning communities (Edwards et al., 2012: 374):

> The teachers prepare the environment to allow light into the room, to flood light from underneath and through objects on the light table, to create shadows on the floor and the wall with an overhead projector. This emphasis comes from a deep understanding of how light calls our attention to changes in colour, form, and motion, to personal perspective, and to a ubiquitous and integrative source that brings disparate objects into eloquent relations.

In documenting a project on light (Vecchi and Giudici, 2004), children described both the light itself and the materials they were exploring in relation to their interactions with light, using phrases such as 'fresco of light, striped light, cold light, uproar of light, spider web light, shady light, light that chases' and my favourite 'light babies' to describe bubble wrap.

When meeting up at forest school, apart from muddy puddles, the most favourite activities were building, lighting and enjoying a fire and wearing head torches when particularly gloomy. In the summary of *Fascination of Fire: Charcoal*, Warden (2012) argues:

> This book about the element of fire, explores the place of fire as a provider. It gives us warmth, a sense of security, a source of fuel that can create and alter materials, such as dough into bread, fruit into jam, or wood into charcoal. Children's fascination with candles on their birthday cake demonstrates that the movement of flames engage children, they are aware from an early age of the hazard of heat.

Rupp (2005: 218) also expresses that

> Fire has a primordial fascination. There's an irresistible and near-mesmerizing appeal to flickering flames . . . It's this universal allure, psychologists believe, that leads children to play with forbidden matches; and it's our ancient obsession with flame that lies at the heart of deliberate fire-setting behavior.

Fire-setting may also suggest that children are increasingly de-linked from natural elements potentially leading to delinquent activity when the opportunity arises but a child has not learned to manage their own risks. Pyle (1993, cited in Kellert, 2002: 141) also suggests that 'the extinction of experience . . . implies a disaffection that can have disastrous consequences'. Fire-lighting is one of the common forest school activities and its mastery is important for children's growing sense of responsibility. During the evolution of human societies, fire was crucial to community, economic and industrial success. Flames, lightning, torches in the dark when switches can be repeatedly on and off, light beams shining through translucent materials, gathering to become warm round a fire, cooking outside, a beautiful sunset or sunrise, the silver glow of moonlight all can give a hint of magic and mystery, much as the first fires, first electricity, first observed volcano eruptions did, and can still provoke awe and wonder.

Air

Children love and become excited by wind and air flow – soon becoming tired as the flow/current is greater than the individual. Children become 'windy' and 'as high as kites' when the wind is strong during outdoor playtimes, but love the feel and force of air upon things. I can remember children becoming excited by making their own very crude kites out of carrier bags and string, running and running, day after day even when the winds had died down, but they learned to create a 'flying current' through their own actions. Children adore 'dizzy play', rolling and tumbling, hanging upside down, jumping, spinning round and round until they fall down, all seemingly mimicking the motion in currents. The gasps babies make when gently buffeted by a strong breeze and the fascination of lying under a tree dappled by sunlight and a soft breeze jostling the leaves all appear to show a connection with what they can only feel on their bodies. It is perhaps when they are older that they begin to see the relational aspects of wind power and enjoy the motion of water affected by wind, washing flapping on a line, and the power of the wind harnessed by boat sails or windmills.

Chawla (2006: 65) cites Gibson and Pick (2000) who 'have shown that people have an innate drive to notice more and more and more about their environment, insofar as it relates to their interests'. I would suggest that joint attention and the relationships that enable these connections are underpinned in the elemental play model. She further outlines:

> the final principle of ecological psychology which helps explain the formative experiences of environmental activists is the importance of learning about the world first hand through one's own actions in it, rather than second hand as others represent it. Nature's newness is composed of established elements and patterns, so that in an approximate way, we can revisit and defend places consecrated by memories of the world as we first knew it.
>
> (2006: 67, 70)

White and Woolley (2014: 31) cite Appleton's (1975) 'habitat theory': 'preferences for particular landscape features are seen to correspond with an evolutionary ancient and deep-seated psychological drive to ensure that our survival needs are met'. It is what the landscape or *place* means to us and the stories, myths and 'monsters' that are created by young children coming to terms with elemental forces that are explored further. It can be a place to play, to be oneself; a place for animals and a place where people walk. A place which has been journeyed over millennia as people travelled for work or grew crops and a place of 'things that have or might be there'. Frye (cited in Rupp, 2005: 349) gives direction to the following chapter, 'earth, air, water and fire are still the four elements of imaginative experience, and always will be'. The natural world, above all, seems to afford possibilities for fantastic thinking, imagination, role play, being scared and coming to terms with being *small* in a large place.

Provocations

- If young children are given elemental experiences – including the tactile, communicative, sensual relationship with people who are modelling the uses and activities with the elements – how might ideas and enquiries emerge and develop?
- To what extent do you recognise children's affinity with earth, water, fire and air?
- In your setting, what are the range of provided opportunities for playing with elements?
- What spontaneous play with water, earth and air have you observed in children? Are there sufficient opportunities in your setting?
- Bringing a fire-pit into the outdoor setting is a safe and interesting activity to routinely offer. Discuss this activity with your team, thinking through any real or perceived challenges.

References

Carson, R. (1956/1998) *The Sense of Wonder*. New York: Harper Collins.

Chawla, L. (2002) Spots of time: manifold ways of being in nature in childhood. In P.H. Kahn, Jr. and S.R. Kellert (eds) *Children and Nature. Psychological, Sociocultural and Evolutionary Investigations*. Cambridge, MA: MIT Press, pp. 199–226.

Chawla, L. (2006) Learning to love the world enough to protect it. www.ntnu.no/documents/10458/19133135/Chawla1.pdf (accessed 14 September 2015).

Edwards, C., Gandini, L. and Forman, G. (2012) Final reflections and guiding strategies for teaching. In C. Edwards, L. Gandini and G. Forman (eds) *The Hundred Languages of Children*, 3rd edn. Westport, CN, and London: Ablex, pp. 357–78.

Faarlund, N. (2007) Defining friluftsliv. In B. Henderson and N. Vikander (eds) *Nature First. Outdoor Life the Friluftsliv Way*. Toronto: Natural Heritage Books.

Kellert, S.R. (2002) Experiencing nature: affective, cognitive, and evaluative development in children. In P.H. Kahn, Jr. and S.R. Kellert (eds) *Children and Nature. Psychological, Sociocultural and Evolutionary Investigations*. Cambridge, MA: MIT Press, pp. 117–52.

Keown, D. (1996) *Buddhism: A Very Short Introduction*. Oxford: Oxford University Press.

Laevers, F. (ed.) (1994) *The Leuven Involvement Scale for Young Children LIS-YC Manual*. Leuven, Belgium: Centre for Experiential Education.

Laevers, F. (2006) *Making Care and Education More Effective Through Wellbeing and Involvement: An Introduction to Experiential Education*. Leuven, Belgium: Centre for Experiential Education.

Malaguzzi, L. (1996) *The Hundred Languages of Children*. Catalogue of the Exhibit. Reggio Emilia, Italy: Reggio Children.

May, P., Ashford, E. and Bottle, G. (2006) *Sound Beginnings: Learning and Development in the Early Years*. London: David Fulton.

Metzner, R. (1999) *Green Psychology. Transforming Our Relationship to the Earth*. Rochester, VT: Park Street Press.

Moore, R.C. and Cosco, N.G. (2003) Developing an earth-bound culture through design of childhood habitats. www.naturallearning.org/earthboundpaper.html (accessed 19 March 2006).

Moran, M. and Brown, V. (2013) Play as a space for possibilities. In A. Woods (ed.) *Child-Initiated Play and Learning. Planning for Possibilities in the Early Years*. London: David Fulton, pp. 83–95.

Reggio Children (1995) *The Fountains*. Reggio Emilia, Italy: Reggio Children.

Reggio Children (1996) *The Hundred Languages of Children*. Catalogue of the exhibit. Reggio Emilia, Italy: Reggio Children.

Rupp, R. (2005) *Four Elements: Water, Air, Fire, Earth*. London: Profile Books.

Utz, G. (n.d.) The water in you. USGS. http://water.usgs.gov/edu/propertyyou.html (accessed 15 December 2015).

Vecchi, V. and Giudici, C. (2004) *Children, Art, Artists: The Expressive Language of Children. The Artistic Language of Alberto Burri*. Reggio Emilia, Italy: Reggio Children.

Warden, C. (2012) *Fascination of Fire. Charcoal*. Auchterarder, Scotland: Mindstretchers.

White, J. (n.d.) *Making a Mud Kitchen*. www.muddyfaces.co.uk/download/Making%20a%20mud%20kitchen.pdf (accessed 29 June 2016).

White, J. (2014) Exploring appropriate outdoor provision for babies and toddlers. In T. Maynard and J. Waters (eds) *Exploring Outdoor Play in the Early Years*. Maidenhead: Open University Press, pp. 42–54.

White, J. and Woolley, H. (2014) What makes a good outdoor environment for young children? In T. Maynard and J. Waters (eds) *Exploring Outdoor Play in the Early Years*. Maidenhead: Open University Press, pp. 29–41.

White, R. and Stoeklin, V. (1998) Children's outdoor play and learning environments: returning to nature. www.whitehutchinson.com/children/articles/outdoor.shtml (accessed 29 June 2016).

Woods, A. (2015) Guiding children's participation. In A. Woods (ed.) *The Characteristics of Effective Learning: Creating and Capturing the Possibilities in the Early Years*. London: David Fulton, pp. 87–102.

Woods, A. (2016) Being involved in levelling. In A. Woods (ed.) *Examining Levels of Involvement in the Early Years: Engaging with Children's Possibilities*. London: David Fulton, pp. 27–42.

CHAPTER

6

The magic chocolate pit

Watching a small child for an extended period of time as she pokes, mixes, transforms, discusses, observes and shares her mud play reinforces an oft observed phenomenon of young children and their imaginative play activity with raw, natural materials. As introduced in Chapter 1, an alternative perspective on children's early development may be seen through an elemental drive to connect with the natural world and all its power, beauty and potential alongside attuned adults. We can support this socio-emotional development and an environment that both allows and encourages instinctive, exploratory and cultural relationships with people, places and things. Working alongside young children, we mediate imaginary play and context.

> **ENCOUNTER: More than mud and water**
>
> I was observing a teaching student in an inner-city school playground. The playground outside the Foundation Unit (three to five year olds) is accessible to children throughout the day. The staff have embraced the notion of following children's interests, learning stories and planning for possible directions in children's learning.
>
> I had spent 10–15 minutes watching the student reading a story to children in a den inside the climbing frame but my attention kept being drawn to a child who crisscrossed the playground many times, stick tucked under her arm, filling a small bucket with water from the outside tap and carrying it to the edge of the playground where she poured it out, then poked and stirred with her stick . . . My attention was held by the children and I went over to watch what they were doing.
>
> She was often joined by two other children, occasionally four children. They all had sticks. I learned later that the sticks had been available to children to make wings. The sticks were being used to prod, dig, mix, stir and poke. She would go and fetch more water to add to the hole they had created. Their body postures and continual

movement around the hole to look at it from a different perspective – sometimes above it, sometimes to the side, sometimes by crouching – suggested a deep level of involvement. They talked about the 'mixture', how wet and sticky, how deep, how they were stirring it. There was a flow of children. Three children were particularly engrossed in this play and shared many exclamations.

Tina: 'We should take this home.'

I asked how she might take this home.

After a moment she replied: 'In an ice-cream cone.'

'What have you made?' I asked.

'A magic chocolate pit.'

They continued to play, with a flow of children watching, joining in, making suggestions and prodding the mixture. I was able to collect my camera and record their play and after a further 15 minutes of watching and adding some commentary went inside. After some moments Tina followed me inside and asked for boots. I had no idea where the school kept them, but in a confident and conspiratorial attitude, she showed me the cupboard, pointed to me where they were and told me that she needed them as her shoes were getting muddy. We had established a relationship through her play and my interest in her play.

I shared this story with an early years practitioner, who reflected how often children associated natural objects/elemental materials with fantastic properties. His big digging pit and at an early years centre had become a 'goblin cave'.

ENCOUNTER: The goblin cave

We found an assortment of objects in the digging pit that often took on a mysterious and magical quality. I encouraged children to speculate about their origin and how they ended up in the digging area. On one particular occasion Donna, a shy three year old who stayed near my side despite her dislike for anything dirty, hit upon a large buried object. It took a group of six children, working collaboratively, to unearth the treasure.

It was ceremoniously washed and it revealed a name and a date. We brought the brick, a collection of stones, worms, pieces of pottery and an old milk bottle inside to look at in closer detail. The stone attracted a lot of attention and the children were interested in the writing. A theory emerged that at night a man crept over the wall and buried it in the ground. This developed into a goblin, a 'good' goblin, who buried it and that accounted for the name on the brick. Children began to draw pictures of what the goblin looked like and role played the goblin flying into nursery on a cloud; however, there were 'bad' goblins and that's why he had to bury it – to stop them from stealing the brick. The brick took on a mystical significance and prompted a fury of storytelling and many evolving theories about the brick's origin.

Source: Mills (n.d.)

Transformation of experience

The goblin story was a meaningful event that sprang from children's imaginations and experience. The 'loose' nature of mud/earth affords children the possibility of using and transforming past and present, real or shared experience into something new – the essence of creativity. Rupp (2005: 351) concurs:

> The four elements are our past. Just as literature grew from ancient fireside tales of heroes, talking animals, and children lost in magical woods, so the intricate edifice of modern science grew from the fundamental four. Water, air, fire, and earth exert their influence at the mental border where the inner world of fantasy and imagination meets the outer world of fact. The four elements are also the template through which we view the world. We are the species, after all, that sometimes manages to see the world in a grain of sand and heaven in a wild flower, to see every common bush afire with God. We see, in fact, what the Greek natural philosophers saw. Sky and ocean, sun and stars. Rain and rocks and mountains.

In our discussion, Mills further makes reference to features such as mounds as being an open invitation for children to create fantasy landscapes beyond the here and now. During a forest school session, I had laid out some simple stick arrows on a familiar path for children to explore and 'find' a large painted pebble. The children immediately considered this to be a dinosaur egg and wanted to take it back to base camp. What I had not noticed, but was quickly associated with the egg, were very large tractor tracks in the field we were walking in. The tracks *were* dinosaur footprints and we spent many moments wondering how big the dinosaur might be and what species. The track and egg were provocations for a boy who was always looking for dinosaurs in the woods; the outcome, however, was spontaneous and, furthermore, a joint and co-constructive adventure. A third encounter ('Rats') provided further connections between young children and rich, imaginary and narrative play.

Knight (2014: 90) suggests:

> There is something elemental and *magical* about a piece of woodland . . . Other wilder places such as beaches also have a *magic* (Knight 2011c). Woods have a significance that reverberates back to the roots of northern and western European culture, when woods covered much of the land. Sacred groves were used for religious rites, but civilisation demanded cultivation and agricultural practices that destroyed the very wildness that early man had claimed as its own.
>
> (Becker, 2011)

ENCOUNTER: 'Rats'

Small woodland animals had been left in the tent for children to discover and decide how they wanted to play with them during the forest school session. A small group of boys (Archie, Sonny and Seb) had taken them to the base of a tree which had a hole at ground level and a mossy mound.

Archie: All the rats will eat him up. They don't live there, they go under; they eat in here. They live under. Do you see this one? (*All boys hold small animals*) That's stopped rats getting them. Yeah, you see? I stopped the rats getting them. Stop the rats! The rats will eat the mud up.
Sonny: The rats will eat the mud up. I got a lady here. Where's my little hole?
Seb: I'm making the hole there.

(*Thomas comes to take photo of hole*)

Sonny: I can make holes. Pow, pow, pow, pow, pow, pow.
Archie: What are you trying to play?
Seb: Now go down my hole. It will be dangerous.
Sonny: It can Seb.
Archie: Are you scary? I'm scary. I scare rats when they come out at night time. They can't scare me either.
Sonny: I will be in my hole. See, it's dangerous. There's a bigger hole. Don't get in there, it's dangerous (*to Sonny*), No, don't – making it wider. No one allowed to go in, only squirrels.

(*Thomas keeps taking photos*)

Sonny: Make it even wider.
Archie: I made a big hole. Aah.
Seb: Wow! That's very massive. We're making a bigger one than you. We only need friends, we are brothers. (*Sonny and Seb are twin brothers*)
Archie: I like big holes 'though, Sonny. There are no chickens in this hole, only nuts. (*Using different voice*) I like nuts. Seb, there are blue nuts. I like pink nuts. I'm struggling in bed. (*In normal voice*) Look at my big hole. It's even bigger than yours.

(*Sonny and Seb are scooping, gouging, digging*)

Archie: I like pink nuts. You like pink nuts? I only like pink nuts and blue nuts.
Seb: Let's go.
Sonny: It's very deep.
Archie: No one come in now, you can come in.
Sonny: There's a very deep hole.
Archie: What are you holding?
Seb: Hedgehog. And we're not letting him in there.

The magic chocolate pit

Archie:	(*new voice*) Hello. I'm a fox. I'm not a fox anymore, I've turned into something else. Can I [the hedgehog] dig? He's got paws.
Seb:	You not allowed.
Archie:	Am I allowed to go in?
Seb:	Not allowed under the tunnel, you will get stuck.
Archie:	We're making holes, James. Where's the fox?
Sonny:	The rabbit is down the hole.
Archie:	How did he get in?

The play lasted thirty minutes. The adult leader remarked that she rarely saw such sustained play at preschool, with children putting their heads together and narrating a story.

Reality and fantasy

The realms of fantasy and ethereal thoughts with actual, tactile engagement and control of the elements again link to spiritual, ritualistic and philosophical development in children; the mastery of matter with a mind full of ideas, questions and possibilities and making the unreal and the real more manageable for developing minds.

On revisiting the school in the first encounter a few months later, I noted with interest the child still playing with her magic chocolate pit, which is wider and deeper, but less sticky as there had been little rain.

Her encounter is an account of creative, reciprocal and reflective relationships with me, as a familiar person (to a minimal extent), but as a leader for a group of children and the school environment as a familiar place and natural objects – as familiar things.

People, places and things are fundamental to Te Whāriki (Ministry of Education, 1996):

> A child learns to talk in a setting where exploration is valued and possible. Learning is about the way in which people perceive and deal with the environment.
>
> (p. 19)

> Children learn through responsive and reciprocal relationships with people, places and things. The learning environment will assist children in their quest for making sense of and finding out about their world if there are active and interactive learning opportunities, with opportunities for children to have an effect and to change the environment.
>
> (p. 43)

In early childhood, children are developing more elaborate and useful working theories about themselves and about the people, places and things in their lives. Many of these theories retain a magical and creative quality, and for many communities, theories about the world are infused with a spiritual dimension.

(p. 44)

Children develop the ability to enquire, research, explore, generate, and modify their own working theories about the natural, social, physical, and material worlds; about Planet Earth and beyond; a relationship with the natural environment and a knowledge of their own place in the environment including myths and legends and oral, non-fictional forms.

(p. 90)

In the third encounter, the boys demonstrate some idea of the natural habitats of woodland animals and what they might eat, but the sustained play seems to have a very different and special quality. In all three encounters, the ideas are wide-ranging and inventive; according to Bettelheim (1976: 45–6) 'as Piaget has shown, the child's thinking remains animistic. To the child, there is no clear line separating objects from living things; and whatever has life has life very much like our own'. Tuan (1978: 21) concurs:

> Human beings identify with animals more closely than with any other aspect of nature. Attachment to rock, water, and plants is derivative because their appeal depends on the degree we see them in animate or anthropomorphic terms. We rely on animals for our sense of self, for our livelihood, as our sentimental outlets.

It does not seem, however, that this animistic tendency to attribute emotions on to animals is limited to animals; the children in these encounters were also transforming objects found in nature to represent both alternative and fantastic realities. Greenman (1988: 29–30) cites Jones and suggests:

> 'To know an object, to know an event, is not simply to look at it and make a mental copy or an image of it. To know an object is to act on it. To know is to modify, to transform the object and to understand the process of this transformation and as a consequence to understand the way the object is constructed' (Piaget, in Jones, 1978: 6). In *To Understand Is to Invent* (1974: 20, 15) Piaget wrote 'To understand is to discover, or reconstruct by discovering' and 'every new truth to be learned [is to] be rediscovered or at least reconstructed by the student, and not simply imparted to him'. '[I]f you watch a child of three, you will see that he is always playing with something. This means that he is working out, and making conscious, something that his unconscious mind had earlier absorbed. Through this outward experience, in the guise of a game, he examines those things and impressions that he has taken in unconsciously. He becomes fully conscious (30) and constructs the future

man, by means of his activities . . . He does it through his hands, by experience, first in play, then through work' (Montessori, 1967: 27).

Kellert (2002: 126) recalls Carson's (1998) idea of the emotional salience of nature and Sebba (1991: 415) who claims that 'the stimuli of the natural environment . . . assault the senses at an uncontrolled strength' (p. 139). In her thought-provoking book *Reconfiguring the Natures of Childhood,* Taylor (2013: 87) cites Meyers (1998) who argues that 'young children's connections to non-human animals develop a sense of belonging to and being responsible for the environment'.

The fox, the hedgehog, the squirrel and the rabbit in the earlier encounter create a world to 'stop the rats'; the brick belongs to the goblin; the stick which has been part of a wing becomes a tool for stirring a magic chocolate mixture; and the pebble is a dinosaur egg left by a dinosaur that has made tracks bigger than six adult boot prints. This is fantastical thinking. It is also demonstrative of Nicholson's (1971) 'loose parts theory'; children will play longer, be more involved, creative and imaginative, when the objects around them, specifically natural objects, can be used according to the child's whims and fancies.

Quality of play

The quality of the play and narrative recalls Vygotsky's notion of the child 'being a head taller in play', and the elemental play concept is nothing if not social constructivist. Moran and Brown (2013: 88–9) suggest

> Given freedom to make choices in their play, both indoors and out (Tovey, 2007), children can be seen as powerful leaders of their own learning, supported by other children and by informed adults as play partners. These constructs of children's learning reflect the theories of Vygotsky (1933) and Bruner (1996) who saw play as a source of development and a tool or process through which children make sense of their world in social interaction. The key word here is 'their'. According to Vygotsky (1978), play creates its own zone of proximal development. We can conceive of this as a zone of possibility, a space where children can exercise their imaginations, rehearse new skills, learn to self-regulate their behaviour and emotions and gain a deeper understanding of contexts and roles.

In outdoor environments and with natural materials, children create their own outcomes of the play in that they use materials in ways that are constructed within the culture of their present play. Today, a stick can be a sword, tomorrow a fishing rod and another day a part of a mud city constructed in a drying puddle swamp. I would argue that children have repeated these themes in play over generations, using the 'loose parts' found in the environment, and it is in this play, Tassinary (1991, cited in Ulrich, 1993: 112) suggests, that 'exposure to such environments may facilitate creative problem solving or high-order cognitive functioning'. Here, we see elements of the playful yet continuous evolution of the human species from nomadic through hunter-gathering to agricultural communities and thence an industrial and technical society. Donaldson (1992: 146) concurs:

> At once it has to be acknowledged that evidence about absolute beginnings is impossible to find. We have seen that, nowadays, children from about the age of three can tackle problems which, though simple, are genuinely in the intellectual construct mode. The ease with which children take to this kind of activity today suggests that it was probably not inaccessible to our quite remote ancestors. Thus when not dealing with profound questions about the nature of reality our forebears would most probably have begun to search for limited kinds of understanding in ways not driven by the desire to achieve anything else at all.

Louv (2012: 53) concurs. He cites (Orians, 2010) who suggests:

> 'There are ghosts of habitats, predators, parasites, competitors, mutualists and conspecifics past, as well as ghosts of meteors, volcanic eruptions, hurricanes, and droughts past'. These ghosts may reside in our genetic attic . . . long-term genetics may lay down a likely pathway for brain development, but the outcome is also determined by the more current environment – by attachment to nurturing human beings.

Elemental layer to ecological systems theory

The link between Louv and Donaldson is that of the suggested elemental layer to Bronfenbrenner's ecological systems theory and a *lens* through which we may see children's development through their relationship with reciprocating adults and the natural environment which also seems to take into account an encounter with an aspect of children's spirituality (Hay and Nye, 2006). Smith (cited in MacNaughton, 2005: 57) is helpful and suggests that the elemental play model may present 'weaving theory and practice to illuminate subjectivities and consider what I bring to bear on my gaze of others'. If the model explores the relationship between children, people, places and things, then it helps us to consider a different truth and dichotomy about children who are highly dependent upon the power that adults are willing to share and children's self-determination: the power of the elements and the sociocultural exploration and learned mastery of the natural environment and the power and truth of children's unique ideas that are rarely vocalised but regularly observed in play. 'By formalizing Elemental Play, we are opening up the discussion amongst those who do influence young children's play experiences. It affords us the possibility of being advocates for the very young child who cannot yet vocalize their possible innate play preference' (Ryder, pers. comm., 2016).

Children, in their exploratory play, Scott (2004: 169) argues,

> have a capacity for mystery-sensing. The ability to be present makes every moment rich in imagination and possibility. Life is not already explained but is experienced as fresh and 'therefore mysterious' (69). This leads to an intense interest in and persistent inquiry about, the nature of things and the workings of the world. It is not clear what makes this capacity spiritual. Being fascinated with the workings of life is part of developing thinking and inquiring skills. A livid sense of mystery can contribute significantly to the formation of imagination and curiosity. Children's minds are capable of flights of imagination and engagement, testing the world for its processes (Gopnik, Meltzoff, and Kuhl, 1999). Levine (1999) argues that children have the ability to function simultaneously in both concrete and imaginative modes of thinking, which opens them to the potential of spiritual experience. Their spiritual experience is both linked to the transcendent and rooted in their daily life events.

Spiritual experience, here, has a connection with fantasy, magic and myth-making. Waller (2007: 400) observed children's themes and patterns of play during research at two settings (a country park and riverside woodland). He recalls:

> As the visits increased, children re-visited and named familiar places – 'The Octopus Tree,' 'Eeyore's Den,' the woods, 'the Top of the World,' 'The Giant's Bed' (of leaves), 'The Goblin's House' and 'Dragonfly Land' (Setting 1) and 'Morgan's Mountain', the 'Crocodile Tree,' 'The Giant's Den,' 'The Trampoline Tree,' and 'The Troll Bridge' (Setting 2).

Many of the accounts in Duckett and Drummond's *Adventuring in Early Childhood Education* (2010) also attest to 'a consistent feature of children's explorations [. . .] has been their theories about creatures, both real and imaginary, that live there' (p. 43), including 'The Glass Crocodile'. Fjørtoft (2001: 114) has also documented the naming of natural playscapes:

> The children's favourite places were named 'The Cone War', 'The Space Ship', and 'The Cliff'. The naming itself is illustrative for the activities taking place there. Free play fostered creative play, and the playscape afforded loose parts and natural objects with materials to play with.

Fairy tales and myths

Once again, imaginative and fantastic scenes are *owned* by the children, some clearly reminiscent of traditional and well-known fairy stories, children's fiction and the explanations adults can give to children when they either find it hard to explain phenomena to children or are offering a magical narrative themselves.

It suggests that natural environments afford more than physical and sensory possibilities to children. Playworld Projects (see Laboratory of Comparative Human Cognition: http://lchc.ucsd.edu/Projects/playworlds.html)

> explore a historically new form of play, one in which adults and children enter into a common fantasy, often using folk stories recorded in books as a key organizing artifact. Playworlds are dramaturgical classroom interventions that focus on emotional experience and aesthetic relation to reality through involving children and adults in staged as well as spontaneous pretend play. These interventions are grounded in the theories of L.S. Vygotsky of Russia, G. Lindqvist of Sweden and Pentti Hakkarainen of Finland, and are designed to enable adults and children to engage in joint pretense as a means of promoting the emotional, cognitive, and social development of both children and adults.

White and Stoeklin (1998) refer to

> Well over 100 studies of outdoor experiences in the wilderness and natural areas show that natural outdoor environments produce positive physiological and psychological responses in humans, including reduced stress and a general feeling of well-being. Children's instinctive feelings of continuity with nature are demonstrated by the attraction children have for fairy tales set in nature and populated with animal characters. The landscapes, trees, and rivers described in fairy tales and myths still exist today.

Steiner Waldorf education remains wedded to the telling of fairy tales and exposing children to a variety of imaginary contexts much as the playworld projects are constructed by adults to enable and encourage joint and playful endeavour. Gilligan (2007: 209, 216, 219), argues, however, that

> elemental landscape [. . .] is hauntingly familiar to me, like a lost song on the wind from ages, dark and dim and mostly forgotten, yet deeply imprinted on my consciousness. Something that the landscape has yielded to its inhabitants, that its inhabitants have passed on down through time, and that somehow, hundreds of years later and thousands of miles distant, made its way into my childhood through books and stories and imaginings. The myths, the sagas, the folktales of the Norse somehow made it through countless land-wars, the Christianization of Europe, the migrations and dispersals of peoples, the humanitarianism of the Rennaissance, the industrial revolution, even the confusion of the post-modern era.

Thoreau writes of wildness as a quality that all things may have, and wilderness as the place where wildness resides. Wilderness, as the 'raw material of life' is essential for life, and further, wildness is essential for wilderness. In wildness, then, is the preservation of the world. Similarly, in friluftsliv philosophy, nature is

> **ENCOUNTER: A bear hunt**
>
> A particular group of children at forest school regularly walked the boundaries of the millennium wood. It was a summer series of sessions; the nettles and grasses were taller than the children and it always seemed a real expedition for the children who enjoyed 'getting lost in the jungle'. One day one of us started singing 'We're going on a bear hunt' and the children picked up the familiar refrains. As they got deeper into the grasses, and invisible apart from the noise of their singing and the motion of their passing by, the bear of the rhyme became a monkey, an alligator, a penguin, a dinosaur, a lion, a bee, a snake – a wide range of species and habitats to imagine, experience and enjoy. On returning from their expedition, the children, once again, focused on the real and miniscule, finding snails and worms and spiders at ground level, a space and place to 'open oneself up for all its qualities and values'.
>
> *Source*: Tordsson (2007: 66)

essential for culture, and without nature culture cannot exist . . . Thoreau further explains that it is not just elemental nature ('wilderness'), but the quality within elemental nature that is essential for the well-being or preservation, of the world.

Friluftsliv encourages us to explore our own cultural roots, far back in time and miles as they may be, and seek to understand how we did in fact co-evolve with the landscapes from which we came.

The children, therefore, easily made the transition from real woodland to extending a familiar rhyme into imagined verses, and then returning to real mini-beasts in the landscape of the forest school. Barrows (1995, cited by White, 2004) suggests that 'Children's instinctive feelings of continuity with nature are demonstrated by the attraction fairy tales set in nature and populated by animal characters have to children'. Taylor (2013: 17–18, 34, 37, 39, 41) argues strongly that these 'instinctive' feelings have everything to do with 'Romantic musings [. . .] with wistful and nostalgic imaginaries and almost nothing to do with the real-life experiences of children.' Her focus is on early and late twentieth-century texts and films which, she argues, reflect 'Rousseau's idealizations of nature' and 'the unfolding traditions of modern 'natural education' and been translated into a range of early childhood nature-related pedagogical practices.' She recognises Rousseau's 'primitive dispositions' of the child (2013 [1762]: 13) has become 'an axiom of modern educational theory' where 'The young child should be left alone to freely explore the external natural world and learn by "his" sensory and physical experiences of it (not adult explanations of it)'. Froebel's gifts, she argues are 'modelled upon his knowledge about the structure and formation of rocks and crystals [. . .] resemble simple open-ended natural play objects-like sticks and stones – to which children are naturally attracted'. Although critical of 'romanticized notions' and their contemporary 'disneyfication' of wilderness, she sees the landscape as having real cultural meaning for children.

Everyday landscapes

Sticks and stones, hills and holes, trees and grasses, puddles and streams, grass and beach, mud, sand and gravel are all part of real-life experiences of childhood, whether children experience these objects in gardens, in nursery environments, on walks and pavements along neighbourhood streets, in bushes of known fields or on beaches when on holidays. All children have a local environment that may be explored. Young children are *very* interested in the things they can pick up, hold, walk along with and throw. They watch tiny insects and larger animals they encounter. They gasp at the wind, and splash in the rain; they marvel at snow and enjoy the sun on their skin. They like to hide in dens of their own making and will clamber into trees they can manage. The majority of these activities are available to them; for some children, the affordance of their local environments can be 'off-limits'. Not all childhood experiences in nature are 'mythical and magical, taking place in "ecstatic" places and functioning as "radioactive jewels buried within us, emitting energy across the years of our life"' (Chawla, 1990: 18, cited in Taylor, 2013: 50). Encounters can be mesmerising nevertheless; stones in a puddle, icicles from a roof gutter, rain swirling in a drain, a spider's web in a shed, and a dandelion clock to name but a few. Tordsson (2007: 66) agrees that

> Nature is a rich storeroom for fantasy, emotions and aesthetic experiences. It holds abundant resources of expressions, symbols and *qualities* [my italics] that interplay with our inner life. By obtaining this immaterial treasure the individual life can be ennobled and sensibility develop.

The everyday fascinations of nature in early childhood may remain within the micro-level of close family relationships but they are a crucial context for the young child, nevertheless. The sharing of narrative, fairy tale and tactile memories are part of our cultural fabric, with generations, for example, chanting the same troll song when walking over a bridge or engaging in a game of 'pooh sticks'. These familial and familiar games may not be as grand as Lewis' (1996, cited in Louv, 2012: 108) 'ancient intuitive threads', but they are able to be encompassed in the elemental play model of shared and reciprocal relationships.

Wattchow (2007: 236) reiterates:

> According to Edward Relph, (1992) '[t]he word "place" is best applied to those fragments of human environments where meanings, activities, and a specific landscape are all implicated and enfolded by each other'. Thus, it is precisely our experiences of a place, which exists in the tension between our sensing bodies and the cultural constructions that govern our interpretations of what a place might mean to us that stands to provide important lessons for education. In other words, we must apprentice ourselves to an experience of place, if place is to become our teacher. In Reggio Emilia, the environment is seen as the 'third teacher'; what is suggested here is that environment might be considered as the second or first teacher within the evolutionary dynamic.

Hay and Nye (2006: 72–4) suggest that 'everyday experience is transcended through imagination [which] seen in their play we may at times be encountering a window on [an] aspect of their spirituality'. They reflect Winnicott's (1971: 73) idea that 'it is in playing and only in playing that the individual child or adult is able to be creative and to use the whole personality, and it is only in being creative that the individual discovers the self'. This discovery, creative, spiritual, elemental if you like, Roszak (1995: 8) suggests is ecological:

> the study of connectedness. As nature around us unfolds to reveal level upon level of structured complexity, we are coming to see that we inhabit a densely connected ecological universe where nothing is 'nothing but' a simple, disconnected, or isolated thing.

Storytelling, myths, imaginative play, transformation of objects, monsters under the bed and in the bushes and make-believe are all part of children's holistic development and inner life. The natural world is an amazing and vast, ever-changing environment that children are constantly coming to terms with through exploratory, hands-on activity. Alongside these real experiences are conversations overheard, stories read, fears anticipated and images absorbed. This is part of cultural exchange and the development of a child being and belonging.

It is children's relationships with *things* and ideas where play evolves, develops, is planned and happens outside any obvious adult interaction or provocation that is examined in the following chapter.

Provocations

- Exploring the boundary between reality and potentiality gives meaning to materials and context. In what ways do you value these experiences for children?
- Where are the 'magic making' and imaginary spaces in your setting?
- What appears to be the difference in the role play and storytelling outside amongst children and any fantastical thinking inside?
- To what extent can children go beyond what is known and create adventures? How do they consider different perceptions of materials and experiment with different dimensions?
- If your children had created a magic chocolate pit, how might you give value to this experience?

References

Bettelheim, B. (1976) *The Uses of Enchantment. The Meaning and Importance of Fairy Tales*. London: Penguin.

Donaldson, M. (1992) *Human Minds: An Exploration*. London: Penguin.

Duckett, R. and Drummond, M.-J. (2010) *Adventuring in Early Childhood Education*. Newcastle-upon-Tyne: Sightlines Initiative.

Fjørtoft, I. (2001) The natural environment as a playground for children: the impact of outdoor play activities in pre-primary school children. *Early Childhood Education Journal* 29(2): 111–17.

Gilligan, D. (2007) Friuftsliv and America. In B. Henderson and N. Vikander (eds) *Nature First. Outdoor Life the Friluftsliv Way*. Toronto: Natural Heritage, pp. 209–20.

Greenman, J. (1988) *Caring Spaces, Learning Places: Children's Environments That Work*. Redmond, WA, USA: Exchange Press, Inc.

Hay, D. with Nye, R. (2006) *The Spirit of the Child*. Revised Edition. London: Jessica Kingsley.

Kellert, S.R. (2002) Experiencing nature: affective, cognitive, and evaluative development in children. In P.H. Kahn, Jr. and S.R. Kellert (eds) *Children and Nature. Psychological, Sociocultural and Evolutionary Investigations*. Cambridge, MA: MIT Press.

Knight, S. (2014) Working with forest schools. In T. Maynard and J. Waters (eds) *Exploring Outdoor Play in the Early Years*. Maidenhead: Open University Press.

Louv, R. (2012) *The Nature Principle: Reconnecting with Life in a Virtual Age*. Chapel Hill, NC: Algonquin.

MacNaughton, G. (2005) *Doing Foucault in Early Childhood Studies: Applying Poststructural Ideas*. Abingdon: Routledge.

Mills, J. (n.d.) Children's relationships with outdoor spaces. Unpublished.

Ministry of Education (1996) *Te Whāriki*. Wellington, NZ: Learning Media.

Moran, M. and Brown, V. (2013) Play as a space for possibilities. In A. Woods (ed.) *Child-Initiated Play and Learning: Planning for Possibilities in the Early Years*. London: David Fulton, pp. 83–94.

Nicholson, S. (1971) How NOT to cheat children: the theory of loose parts. *Landscape Architecture* 62: 30–4.

Roszak, T. (1995) Where psyche meets Gaia. In T. Roszak, M.E. Gomes and A.D. Kanner (eds) *Ecopsychology. Restoring the Earth: Healing the Mind*. San Francisco: Sierra Club, pp. 1–17.

Rupp, R. (2005) *Four Elements: Water, Air, Fire, Earth*. London: Profile.

Scott, D. (2004) Spirituality and children: paying attention to experience. In H. Goelman, S. Marshall and S. Ross (eds) *Multiple Lenses, Multiple Images: Perspectives on the Child across Time, Space, and Disciplines*. Toronto: University of Toronto Press, pp. 168–196.

Taylor, A. (2013) *Reconfiguring the Natures of Childhood*. London: Routledge.

Tordsson, B. (2007) What is friluftsliv good for? Norwegian friluftsliv in a historical perspective. In B. Henderson and N. Vikander (eds) *Nature First. Outdoor Life the Friluftsliv Way*. Toronto: Natural Heritage, 62–74.

Tuan, Y.-F. (1977) *Space and Place: The Perspective of Experience*. Minneapolis and London: University of Minnesota Press.

Tuan, Y.-F. (1978) Children and the natural environment. In I. Altman and J.F. Wohlwill (eds) *Human Behaviour and Environment, Advances in Theory and Research. Vol. 3: Children and the Environment*. New York: Plenum Press, pp. 5–32.

Ulrich, R.S. (1993) Biophilia, biophobia, and natural landscapes. In S.R. Kellert and E.O. Wilson (eds) *The Biophilia Hypothesis*. Washington, DC: Shearwater, pp. 73–137.

Waller, T. (2007) The trampoline tree and the swamp monster with 18 heads: outdoor play in the foundation stage and foundation phase. *Education 3–13* 35(4): 393–407.

Wattchow, B. (2007) Experience of place: lessons on teaching, cultural attachment to place. In B. Henderson and N. Vikander (eds) *Nature First. Outdoor Life the Friluftsliv Way*. Toronto: Natural Heritage, pp. 235–45.

White, R. (2004) Young children's relationship with nature: its importance to children's development & the earth's future. www.whitehutchinson.com/children/articles/children nature.shtml (accessed 13 April 2007).

White, R. and Stoeklin, V. (1998) Children's outdoor play and learning environments: returning to nature. www.whitehutchinson.com/cgi-bin/printer.cgi?p=/children/articles/outdoor.shtml (accessed 25 April 2006).

Winnicott, D. (1971) *Playing and Reality*. London and New York: Routledge.

CHAPTER

7

Playing with things: children's ideas and projects

In earlier chapters, young children's developing relationship with the people they grow up with, and the contextual environment they develop within has been explored. This chapter considers the playfulness of children's learning and the *disposition* to be ready, willing and able to pursue a project or schema of ideas actively 'observed to be a sort of "fingering over" of the environment in sensory terms, a questioning of the power of materials as a preliminary to the creation of higher organization of meaning' (Cobb, 1977: 48). As described in Woods (2015: 64):

> This 'fingering over' (Cobb, 1977) is suggestive of Piaget's theory of schematic play, and a project or learning inquiry appears to be driven by a desire to make sense of a thing or idea, repeatedly. Rinaldi (in Dahlberg and Moss, 2005: 106–7) considers 'The word "project" evoke[ing] the idea of a dynamic process, an itinerary. It is sensitive to the rhythms of communication and incorporates the significance and timing of children's investigations and research'.

Projects

In early discussions with Debbie Ryder, we *troubled* the notion that very young children can have projects. A project is, by its name, an idea that a person can project (forward plan); it can also be an idea that is subsequently woven in and observed into a set or series of activities. This can be observed in a child who has a significant interest in an action, idea or resource and also supported by an attuned adult. We began talking and arguing about what very young children seem to be drawn to and Debbie, working with under-twos, had observed three distinct actions:

- attuned adults;
- safe and happy places;
- an object or action with an object they repeatedly explore.

Repeated exploration can be defined as schematic play, identified by Piaget, and researched by Athey, Bruce and Nutbrown. We can define a schema being an observed repeatable set of behaviours exercised by a child as they try to make sense of something; for example, why things go round, what happens when we throw things, how things fit together, enveloping, transporting and covering objects. These are quite mathematical and observable schemas, but we had noticed a much more natural and emotional basis for young children's play, not so easily measurable, perhaps, as vertical constructions or long snakes of animals and cars. Natural materials and forces appeared to attract children and satisfy them for extended periods, both outdoors and indoors, particularly those we have already defined as loose materials. Jess, a forest school leader has noted

> [the children] tend to revisit the things they have enjoyed most week after week, or talk about them the most to their parents or me. It differs for each child but the common themes are playing with mud, sticks, paddling in the stream and eating snacks!

Open-ended objects allow the child to establish a clear sense of self as protagonist. As children experiment with the shape, texture and fabric of particular objects, and what they can do with it, they discover their own physical strength as well as make connections with other objects they have explored. Natural materials, particularly outside, have different qualities to those presented inside. The majority of indoor toys and objects are hard, often shiny and have similar weights; natural materials offer diversity of weight, malleability and less uniform qualities. Open-ended natural and found objects stimulate ideas and act as play partners in children's inquiries. Explorations of the natural elements within the play environment stimulate further connections with previous encounters that have occurred culturally in the life of the child. Fond memories are then attached to these learning experiences, which are then 'stowed' away for future reference. As the young child develops, they are drawn to a more diverse source of materials and resources, drawing upon what we may call their cognitive well-being, or spirit, but memories will be called upon, and they will experience a sense of coming together of self and other, absorbed in body, mind and place.

We had seen young children feeling very comfortable with particular and familiar adults in early years settings, and those who found contentment and security in a familiar place or play area; we also could observe whether children enjoyed and repeatedly played with certain objects and assume the role of active participants. An attachment to an idea, question or inquiry was perhaps more difficult to infer and measure and perhaps a reason why mathematical activity has been more the focus of schematic observations.

Holt (1989: 95) suggests:

> Children are born passionately eager to make as much sense as they can of things around them. The process by which children turn experience into knowledge is exactly the same, point for point, as the process by which those who become scientists make scientific knowledge. Children observe, they wonder, they speculate, and they ask themselves questions. They think up possible answers, they make theories, they hypothesize, and then they test theories by asking questions or by further observations or experiments or reading.

Ryder, writes about a project in 2005. The centre, close to a beach in New Brighton, Christchurch was focus for 'Above and Below the Sea'.

The project continued with many children connecting the film *Finding Nemo* to the project, creating driftwood mobiles and involving the community in beach-combing and display work.

ENCOUNTER: Michael

Michael was a quiet four year old who tended to sit on the peripheral of a lot of centre activities. The context for Michael and Corrina's (his mum) increasing participation was through Tania (parent) who had been actively involved with the sea project. One afternoon Tania and her daughter, Kylie, were looking at the display board with Michael and Corrina. Tania was talking to Corrina about taking Michael to the beach, encouraging them to go and collect shells for Michael to make his own mobile. Corrina indicated that she was not keen. Tania encouraged 'Go on, it only takes a few minutes to collect shells and some seaweed!' Both mothers continued to talk about the beach as they and their children left the centre for the day.

A few days later, I heard Michael talking with his grandmother about going to the beach. I talked with them about finding unusual things on the beach. He was insistent to 'Nan' that they go soon. The next time I saw Michael, he was with his mum. They both came and found Katrina (practitioner) and myself to show us the things that Michael and his grandmother had collected. In he came with a box that was almost too big for him to carry – he very proudly put the box down and we started to look through the things he had picked up. There were large pieces of seaweed, pods, shells, driftwood and crab shells; then there was a sea sponge, shells with hair growing out of them and beach flowers. Michael was very proud of his treasures.

Was there a meaningful connection for Michael between his home life and the experience in the centre? I asked Corrina: 'What happened to the beach treasures once you and Michael got home?'

'When we finally got round to it we put the goodies from the beach into a big blue pot that we have outside the garage. It is decorated with shells and driftwood.'

We can argue that the project was *provoked* by adults in the centre, but in a later, shared, learning story, Debbie recalls Corrina's answer when she also said that it had taken a week to display the beach treasures at home because Dad was 'fixing wheels' in the garage; fixing wheels was a fascination for Michael. As he became more involved in the centre, he was encouraged to follow this interest and develop it into a project which he led. Fixing wheels was one of Michael's 'things'. Here, we begin to see connections between Michael, Corrina, his Nan and Tanya (people), the Centre and the beach (place) and the treasures – both natural beach objects and the wheels in his Dad's garage as contextual *things* in and of his childhood.

A child's project can be within its own time frame. An enduring, deep level interest may be observed in young children through into adolescence, supported by adult interest, not necessarily intervention, and encouraged to emerge. This is most noticeable in one's own children because of the familiar, family context and a *playful* interest sometimes becomes a life-long recreation or career influence. In our settings, these longer-term projects or inquiries can be less noticeable because of competing interests, pressures of external demands of our own and the children's time, and because of frequent changes in adult personnel; children attending Steiner schools may be said to benefit from less transition between adult teachers. We should be able to observe, however, the constancy of interests *and* the way that children approach both their own chosen tasks and those framed by adult-led direction, and to what extent we can capitalise and enhance a powerful disposition to learn. It is in Reggio Emilia where long-term projects are most evident:

> Always and everywhere children take an active role in the construction and acquisition of learning and understanding. So it is that in many situations, especially when one sets up challenges, children show us they know how to walk along the path to understanding. Once children are helped to perceive themselves as authors or inventors, once they are helped to discover the pleasure of inquiry, their motivation and interest explode.
>
> (Malaguzzi, in Gandini, 1998: 67)

Curiosity and exploration: dispositions for effective learning

Children want to experiment, to find their own way, so there is a science of curiosity, and one can argue that in natural elements and forces, the affordance for curiosity is great. Gibson (1988: 7) suggests that

> Exploratory behaviour during the first year of life occurs as a sequence of phases that build the infant's knowledge of the permanent features of the world, of the predictable relations between events, and of [her] own capacities for acting on objects and intervening in events.

Carr (2001) has outlined five features of participation in the learning process; the dispositions are:

- taking an interest;
- being involved;
- persistence with difficulty or uncertainty;
- communicating with others;
- taking an increasing responsibility.

She expands by noting that children can be seen to be ready, willing and able to demonstrate these dispositions, and a child begins to recognise that one's actions are part of oneself as well as that actions produce effects; this can include questions and problem-solving which can be part of an internalised process or inquiry. Wattchow and Brown (2011: 45) cite Kolb (1984), who also saw components for making meaning: concrete experience, reflective observation, abstract conceptualisation and active experimentation. It may be argued, therefore, that a child can project previous ideas and actions and return to a task with a new plan or inquiry; Csíkszentmihályi might call this 'being in flow' and Laevers 'like a fish in water'. Katz (2001, in Brooker, 2011: 85) concludes:

> Children, all children, are born with the disposition to make sense of their experiences. This is also what scientists do – make sense of experiences by experimenting, by utilizing the scientific process. You can see this disposition even in babies. A 4-month-old will drop a spoon and watch as Grandma picks it up – over and over again. She is a scientist, testing her environment to see what happens.

Physical playfulness with materials is a natural part of development, particularly for children but also for adults who have and will need to explore materials in order to understand, use and develop them for actual and future needs. We can almost *see* a child thinking 'What does this thing do?' and 'What can I do with

---

ENCOUNTER: Cassie's ideas

Cassie, aged six-and-a-half, recounts her afternoon playtime at school:

Cassie: Mummy, I threw a stick up into the sky.
Mum: Did you, didn't it come back down?
Cassie: Yes and it had fluff on it.
Mum: ...what was the fluff?
Cassie: Cloud.
Mum: Wow!

Here, Cassie is transforming her emerging understanding of clouds through imaginative ideas.

this thing?' This is rarely vocalised, but can be observed through expression and body language or in quite abstract thoughts.

Needham (in Waller et al., 2011: 57) suggests:

> Knowledge, it is argued, is not something that exists preformed to be discovered, it is rather developed through the evolution of human activity. Humanity has developed both physical tools and mental tools through experience and the desire to achieve certain goals. Knowledge will always be evolving in the light of what we seek to do and will always build upon the cultural practices of the past. We develop through learning to participate in the use of physical tools [for example] (writing materials) and mental tools (language) that are available to us to adapt the environment in which we find ourselves.

Problem-solving and inquiry

It is this adaptation and cultural disposition that underpins an elemental concept of inquiry. One of the parents at Little Muddy Boots responded to a question about her previous experience of the outdoors by saying

> [it is] an adventure, made up stories, building etc; finding that some ways didn't work and problem-solving to make it work. I think it had a huge influence on how I look at problems today . . . I seem unable to give up until the job is done.

A working definition of elemental play might be:

> children exploring the 'I am' and 'I can' and 'should I' through ideas and notions and inquiries which is the elemental process of finding out about self in relation to people, places and things, through *their* discovery of the natural environment.

Their new knowledge is a re-creation of the discoveries made over human time and recognised by those adults who are attuned to the development of play and children. Recreation is a form of play and recognition is coming to know a thing or idea *again*. We play or problem-solve whenever we try to connect new with habituated information. We all wonder about the elements, are in awe and have to master them to survive. Elemental play, therefore, can be defined as an instinctive, human and cultural disposition.

Vasta (1992: 41) cites Finkelstein and Ramey (1977) and Ramey and Finkelstein (1978), suggesting that

> Infants who experience success in controlling environmental events become more attentive to their own behaviour and more competent in learning new

efficacious responses, than do infants for whom the same environmental events occur regardless of how they behave.

Ulrich (cited in Wattchow and Brown, 2011: 110) supports this by stating that

> 'Higher order' cognitive functioning involves integrating diverse material or associating in a flexible way previously unrelated information or concept [and] required for forming remote associations and for creative problem solving. The notion that exposure to natural settings may enhance high-order cognitive functioning is proposed tentatively as a 'candidate' category of biophilic responding.

We know that Vygotsky suggested that children 'play a head above themselves' in self-motivated, imaginative play. It is incumbent on us to afford possibilities for active learning, for children to become 'life-theorizers' (Hedges, cited in Brooker, 2010: 30). How the child performs, 'the way an activity or practice is carried out is highly important for its developmental effect' (van Oers, in Edwards et al., 2010: 198), underpinning 'the idea of "learning dispositions" [as] one of the newest and most powerful theoretical constellations to be found in early childhood education' (Brooker, 2011: 83). Here again, we can see that

> The influence of play on a child's development is enormous. Play in an imaginary situation is essentially impossible for a child under 3 in that it is a novel form of behaviour liberating the child from constraints. The behaviour of a very young child . . . is determined by the conditions in which the activity takes place. A study by Lewin on the motivating nature of things for a very young child concludes that *things* dictate to the child what he must do.
>
> (Vygotsky, 1978: 96)

Ensuring that a positive and curious attitude towards finding things out through practice/error/practice/achievement is how we all learn from the youngest baby to an older person faced with a new cognitive/technical challenge: we use what we know and adapt to acquire a different understanding.

Experiential education

Dewey's ideas are recalled here:

> the person in Dewey's philosophy requires involvement with process, time, space, and histories, since forces and qualities remain lifeless unless elicited through interaction in the events and situations of the environment – an environment that exists, is there, while also is created and transformed through interaction. The person is 'in' as well as 'of' the environment.
>
> (Cuffaro, 1995: 16)

> **ENCOUNTER: Penny and the snails**
>
> 1. Asking Penny why she liked snails so much. She said it was the circles, her favourite being the brown, white and black stripes. Ah, I replied, the stripe pattern was a spiral. 'Yes, I like the spirals.' Penny sustained her interest in snails, repaying the adults with evidence of deep engagement.
> 2. For the past three weeks, Penny has set about finding, holding and examining snails. She also picks up slugs and now knows that slugs do not live in shells but excrete slime to enable them to move. She finds very tiny snails and those with distinct patterns on their shells; she begins to notice the spiral pattern. When she picks them up, the snails go back into their shells and she wants them to crawl . . . I make a suggestion that if she holds her hands still, the snail will usually emerge through warmth and stillness. Penny is too busy on the hunt for more snails and often deposits the found snails in my hand to 'warm them up'. Once emerged, she usually places them on a tree for safety and then is surprised at how far they can climb. Last week, Michael, caught up in her interest, spent a long time creating a nested bed for the snails and they both placed all the found snails on a log disc before covering them in dry leaves.
>
> *Source*: Woods (2015: 91)

Being in and of the environment is part of the forest school experience. Penny had been visiting the millennium wood for a few weeks and was very confident to pursue her own ideas. She could often be found 'grubbing' around the undergrowth and looking under logs.

Experiential education is the opportunity to 'go with the flow'; spiral patterns seen in shells, slime on hands, a snail's energetic climb; unplanned but an anticipated possibility, and an adult 'ready, willing and able' to support and follow a child's interest. 'The project [experiential education] still in progress, is regarded in Flanders and in the Netherlands as one of the most influential innovative movements of the nineties in the field of early childhood and primary education' (Laevers, 2003a: 7). Laevers' (Laevers, 2003b: 13) concern is that 'too many opportunities to sustain children's development remain unused'. This is noticeable in many outdoor environments where fewer practitioners can be observed fully participating in wild and imaginative play. It remains curious that for many early years practitioners, the play of children outside can be one of 'watchful concern' rather than participative playfulness and joint exploration. This perceived challenge is considered in Chapters 8 and 9.

High levels of involvement

Laevers (cited in Robson, 2012: 116) states that 'involvement only occurs in the small area in which the activity matches the capabilities of the person that is in the "zone of proximal development"'. Levels of involvement, like ZPD are part of our early years lexicon and are considered in greater depth in Woods (2016). Elemental play gives us a lens through which we can see a child's actual development and their struggle to understand the world around them. Recent ecological, biophilic theories would suggest that in their earliest, natural explorations, we glimpse possible future development providing that the relational context is afforded to them, sustaining 'intergenerational traditions and community life that have formed the basis of different cultures and which have provided ecologically [sound] practices' (Wattchow and Brown, 2011: 43).

Kimes Myers (1997: 5–6) is persuasive:

> When theories are woodenly applied by those who try to emulate the initial theory-builders, the richness of a particular child's play and the uniqueness of how that child engages in the activities of early childhood can often be lost. This occurs when theories and research findings are dogmatically applied and, as a result, lose the spiritedness, wonder, aliveness, and relevance that gave birth to them in the first place. This often happens because we inadvertently allow theories to become blinders rather than lenses. Our use of theory may result in missing the 'something new' that could be bubbling on the edge of the subject (not the object) of all such effort; that is, we often miss the child.

Such exploration on the margins of what we know allows those who live and work with young children to accept the position of becoming informal researchers even as they explore this *edge*; that is, they might be investigating what we still don't know even as they ask questions related to the children in their care; elemental play has the potential to move us beyond that inherited from those who came before.

Having identified the needs of an individual child and how he preferred to be settled outdoors when his mum left (see Chapter 3), Debbie Ryder (2005) introduced more natural resources to the indoor environment.

Ideas and feelings

Children's play preferences, their inquiries and their explorations can be deeply expressed through relationships with people, places and things; things can be actual objects or abstract ideas formed through their learning inquiries. The environmental and emotional *affordances* of Debbie's centre and the careful research of children's attitudes towards an active exploration of materials combined to support the development of strong and robust characteristics of effective learning and promote children's own projects or learning inquiries. Ryder's actions reflect Wattchow and Brown (2011: 43) recalling Dewey who felt

> that education should provide an emancipatory, democratic encounter with learning rather than a passive and disengaged experience controlled by others. Some form of reflection, [and] the learner constructs their understanding of the meaning of their experiences.

Playing with things: ideas and projects

ENCOUNTER: Throwing out the plastic

A search in the cupboard found a beautiful variety of stones and shells. These were then added to the everyday items – it was interesting to observe the young children as they encountered the small shells and stones – would they put them in their mouths? It seemed though that the children were far more interested in these natural materials than just to put them in their mouths, they wanted to experience what they felt like, sounded like etc.

Due to a bad patch in the weather and an ever increasing interest in the shells and stones, we were beginning to bring our outside environment inside for the children to experience and they became a normal part of our inside materials. We were noticing that these natural materials were holding the children's interest where the plastic toys were not. It was at this stage that we decided we wanted natural and everyday materials to not be just a part of the programme, but to also be the programme we offered children. We concluded, after a month of observation, we wanted to take all the plastic equipment out of the centre, and would work with natural and suitable wooden materials. At this point, shells and stones were aesthetically displayed, the environment arranged in a wonderfully welcoming way for children and adults alike – more and more children and adults are being drawn to the infant and toddler area.

Outside, we realised that we could no longer just rely on the sandpit, grass and plastic slide to provide stimulating experiences; major physical changes needed to occur if the outside environment would provoke experiences of inquiry to occur in the same way as was now occurring inside.

Across from the pebble pit is an area for exploration and climbing, natural logs, boulders, and tree stumps provide for highly skilled climbing challenges. The bridge serves as an area of transition between the small concrete area for bouncing balls etc. through to the natural environment. A seat has been positioned so that children and adults can share some time together.

The following learning story is just one of many that describe our new environment in action.

It was near the end of the day and a few children came outside with me as I was clearing things away. Dawn and I noticed the way that the environment was offering Keiran a new challenge as he climbed up and over the large log to get into the sandpit. He stayed in the sandpit for an extended period of time as he explored the texture of the sand. As he got up he thought about how he could get out, and it was then that he wandered over to the end where there is a gap between the log and the fence. Then something caught his attention – it was our new sculpture that I had placed outside by the tree. Keiran crawled over to it and stared at it for a short time, not too sure as to what it was – but it certainly caught his attention. He then crawled past the sculpture to settle in his favourite spot – amongst the pebbles! We played together with the pebbles, lifting them up high and trickling them through our fingers, and listening while they dropped back down again. We repeated this action for a while. He enjoyed the feel of the pebbles under his feet and spent some time kicking his legs

> back and forth – digging his feet further into the pebbles to 'feel' them even more! As we continued to play together, Keiran began making really loud noises – as if he was calling out, he could hear the older children playing in the over-twos – was he calling out to them? Keiran would look around and then call out again, enjoying using his voice in this new way – I wonder what he was saying? I wonder if he was relating to his prior experience of our recent trip to the beach with his mum and preschool friends. We know that an effective curriculum is one which links prior 'known' experiences that happen outside the centre, for example, our trip to the beach, with experiences within the centre – shells, pebbles, driftwood. Then Keiran heard a voice he recognised, and as he looked towards the inside he saw his mum – a big smile went on his face as he recognised who it was, and off he went to greet her!

Our role, therefore, is to help children make connections within the learning environment and with other children who have similar but distinct interests. Robinson (1977: 48) asks of us:

> Do we learn more about the nature of a tadpole by preserving it in formalin, or by watching it grow up into a frog? The analogy is inexact: the tadpole has no option, while the patterns that human childhood can take, the paths that it's unfolding can follow, are infinitely variable. Still, that variety is always limited by a number of cultural and environmental factors.

This is explored further in the next chapter where provision for children can be designed into an environment as well as allowing for the possibilities of spontaneous exploration of the elements and play with natural materials.

Katz (1993) writes with authority about learning dispositions: 'The disposition to investigate, may be thought of as inborn. When children's experiences support the manifestation of a disposition with appropriate scaffolding and environmental conditions, the disposition is likely to become robust.' Michael (2005: 112) states we will then nurture

> Children finding their places in the natural world, children who know that water doesn't just come from a tap, who can name the plants and animals around them, understand the challenges of living sustainably on the earth, and gain the tools and imagination to address those challenges. You get children who know their 'ecological addresses'.

Children who have this robust environmental awareness, 'an ark loaded', and a naturalist intelligence are less likely, therefore, to develop biophobic behaviour and treat nature 'as something to be controlled and dominated rather than loved and preserved' (White and Stoeklin, 1998). Biophilia and biophobia are social constructs and a relatively recent explanation for what appears to be a cultural concern about communities less able to connect fully with their local environments. It has been argued in this chapter that young children are naturally curious, this curiosity is enhanced when encountering new sensations and experiences. Outdoor environments offer a greater diversity and richer quality of objects to explore and possibilities to imagine. Given time, context, relationships and opportunity, these possibilities become ideas and we can observe children returning to and re-creating playful behaviours. In other words, children are capable of projecting past experiences onto new ideas and unique activity, having created their own zone of proximal and contextual development.

Provocations

- How might it be possible to investigate babies' and toddlers' active learning from the perspective of watching for ideas connected to people, places and things and whether prolonged inquiry is the idea or the emerging understanding of the child's relationship with one or a combination of these?
- In what ways can we exploit children's innate exploration and curiosity of natural materials?
- If young children are afforded elemental experiences – including the tactile, communicative, sensual relationship with people who are modelling the uses and activities with the elements – how will ideas and inquiries emerge and progress?
- What theories do you recognise as supporting an elemental play philosophy within an infant and toddler environment?
- To what extent are the materials in your setting in themselves a means for expression and communication of one's thoughts and feelings to self and others?
- How far would you feel able to investigate babies' and toddlers' active learning through the lens of their ideas and how they are forming connections to people, places and things?
- Consider writing narrative observations focusing on children *in their element* playing with things, things in places, things with people and things in places with people.
- How might you define a project? To what extent is this different from an abiding interest?
- Are very young children able to have projects in mind?
- Proposals, questions and ideas for projects often come from children. In what ways do you enable these proposals to become part of the curriculum offer?

References

Brooker, L. (2010) Learning to play in a cultural context. In P. Broadhead, J. Howard and E. Wood (eds) *Play and Learning in the Early Years*. London: Sage, pp. 27–42.

Brooker, L. (2011) Developing learning dispositions for life. In T. Waller, J. Whitmarsh and K. Clarke (eds) *Making Sense of Theory and Practice in Early Childhood: The Power of Ideas*. Maidenhead: Open University Press, pp. 83–98.

Carr, M. (2001) *Assessment in Early Childhood Settings: Learning Stories*. London: PCP.

Cobb, E. (1977/1993) *The Ecology of Imagination in Childhood*. Putnam, CT: Spring Publications.Cuffaro, H.K. (1995) *Experimenting with the World: John Dewey and the Early Childhood Classroom*. New York: Teachers College Press.

Gandini, L. (1998) History, ideas, and basic principles: an interview with Loris Malaguzzi. In C. Edwards, L. Gandini and G. Forman. (eds) *The Hundred Languages of Children*, 2nd edn. Westport, CN, and London: Ablex, pp. 27–72.

Gibson, E.J. (1988) Exploratory behaviour in the development of perceiving, acting and the acquiring of knowledge. *Annual Review Psychology* 39: 1–42.

Holt, J. (1989) *Learning All the Time*. New York: Perseus.

Katz, L.G. (1993) *Dispositions: Definitions and Implications for Early Childhood Practice*. Eric Clearing House on Elementary and Early Childhood Education [ED363454], Urbana, Illinois.

Kimes Myers, B. (1997) *Young Children and Spirituality*. London: Routledge.

Laevers, F. (2003a) Introduction. In F. Laevers and L. Heylen (eds) *Involvement of Children and Teacher Style: Insights from an International Study on Experiential Education*. Studia Paedagogica 35. Leuven, Belgium: Leuven University Press, pp. 7–12.

Laevers, F. (2003b) Making care and education more effective through well being and involvement. In F. Laevers and L. Heylen (eds) *Involvement of Children and Teacher Style: Insights from an International Study on Experiential Education*. Studia Paedagogica 35. Leuven, Belgium: Leuven University Press, pp. 13–24.

Michael, P. (2005) Helping children fall in love with the earth: environmental education and the arts. In M.K. Stone and Z. Barlow (eds) *Ecological Literacy. Educating Our Children for a Sustainable World*. San Francisco: Sierra Club Books, pp. 111–25.

Needham, M. (2011) Using activity theory to examine the factors shaping the learning partnership in a parent and child 'stay and play' session. In T. Waller, J. Whitmarsh and K. Clarke (eds) *Making Sense of Theory and Practice in Early Childhood*. Maidenhead: McGraw Hill/Open University Press, pp. 54–68.

Robinson, E. (1977) *A Study of the Religious Experience of Childhood*. Oxford: Religious Education Centre.

Robson, S. (2012) *Developing Thinking and Understanding in Young Children. An Introduction for Students*, 2nd edn. London: Routledge.

Ryder, D. (2005) Elemental play: more than sand and water. Unpublished.

van Oers, B. (2010) Children's enculturation through play. In L. Brooker and S. Edwards (eds) *Engaging Play*. Maidenhead: Open University Press, pp. 195–209.

Vasta, R. (ed.) (1992) *Six Theories of Child Development: Revised Formulations and Current Issues*. London: Jessica Kingsley.

Vygotsky, L. (1978) *Mind in Society. The Development of Higher Psychological Processes*. Cambridge, MA: Harvard University Press.

Wattchow, B. and Brown, M. (2011) *A Pedagogy of Place. Outdoor Education for a Changing World*. Clayton, Vic., Australia: Monash University.

White, R. and Stoeklin, V. (1998) Children's Outdoor play and Learning Environments: Returning to Nature. http://www.whitehutchinson.com/cgi-bin/printer.cgi?p=/children/articles/outdoor.shtml (accessed 25 April 2006).

Woods, A. (2015) Children's engaging interests. In A. Woods (ed.) *The Characteristics of Effective Learning. Creating and Capturing the Possibilities in the Early Years*. London: David Fulton, pp. 56–70.

Woods, A. (ed.) (2016) *Examining Levels of Involvement in the Early Years: Engaging with Children's Possibilities*. London: David Fulton.

CHAPTER

8

Playing naturally: outdoors and inside

There are children who want to run and those who want to hide or find a dappled shelter to read; those who climb and some who root around under logs to search for insects. Many children transport water to pour, splash and mix and some dig and tunnel in sand and mud; others use a space to wander and engage alone or with others in free-flow imaginary play. There are children who practise skills such as skipping, throwing and balancing or rolling down slopes and those who use real tools; others develop acute sensory awareness. We care for children who may first encounter seasonal and metallurgical conditions such as fog, rain, ice, snow, shade from bright sunshine, strong breezes and frosty cobwebs with us. As adults preparing for young children's possibilities, our outdoor environments need to provide for the unique learning journeys of each child whilst recognising their crucial connections to people, places and things. This relationship is woven through the experiential nature of the habitats we provide, developed through the theoretical play constructs we have absorbed in training and in observations. These theoretical constructs will be expanded further in the final chapter. Here, a consensus of ideas, design, resource provision and pedagogy will be examined that support both the key ideas behind the notion of elemental play and how our *prepared* environments can begin to meet children's natural exploration of the world around them.

As children's everyday horizons widen to encompass new relationships, environment and experiences, play activity becomes more refined and focused on form and function, so children's spontaneous playful encounters with natural materials can become less of an everyday occurrence. It can become limited to recreational activities, holidays and *free* time events, when and where the context is more favourable than in their regular early days of puddle splashing, scooping stones and digging mud. It is interesting that as adults with young children, we often try to re-create the natural play of our own early childhood, but as many warn, this may become less likely in cultural contexts where families and community perceive the freedom to play outdoors as dangerous, dirty and chaotic, and the opportunity to freely explore is restricted by the way in which green space is used. Fewer children in each generation have the freedom of everyday access to natural spaces outside backyards and gardens due to the built environment, traffic and work/life balance of families. Some children do not have gardens or outdoor playspace in which to experience the messiness or minutiae of life, or of weather and the effect of elemental forces. Kahn (2002) talks of environmental, generational amnesia, preceding Louv (2012) who argues that a 'nature-deficit-disorder' is both prevalent in adults and children, and how our 'vicarious' experience of nature has become increasingly at arms distance and second hand; however, it is also noticeable that over the last fifteen to twenty years, the interest in outdoor experience, forest schools, woodland play and outdoor classrooms for young children is the focus of many conferences, associations, training courses and book chapters, particularly in the English context. There is a growing interest in research and ideas from Scandinavia, Australia, Canada and New Zealand, and in the sustained approaches followed by Te Whãriki and Reggio Emilia practitioners. What is more interesting to consider is the *border crossing* of disciplines: psychology and eco-psychology, environmental activism and postmodern socio-culturalism. The ideas of Froebel, Pestalozzi, Steiner, Montessori, McMillan and Isaacs sit alongside the practice of frilutisliv, the Maori belief in Mana (spirit), the forest kindergartens of Denmark, and a number of nurseries and primary schools that have introduced and incorporated outdoor experiences for young children. These experiences reflect Bronfenbrenner's ecological systems theory of continual and dynamic influences on the development of the child within a family, community and global environment.

Elemental play

Here, it seems imperative to summarise key points from the preceding seven chapters before acknowledging the number of current authors who are writing about early years play outdoors: the influential philosophers held in such high esteem by practitioners and whose tradition remains strongly visible in the environments we create in our diverse provision, and a consensus of views about what we should provide to enhance and enrich children's lives. A brief but not exhaustive list of design features is given and considered alongside key aspects of elemental play ideas and a discussion of how we might increase the presence of natural materials indoors and outside in small spaces is suggested. Towards the end of the chapter, some of the challenges facing many practitioners are presented and provocations offered for reflection.

The notion of elemental play affirms that children seem to have a preference for areas rich in natural resources. There is an observable dynamic interplay of nature and nurture and children are drawn to and demonstrate high levels of well-being and involvement when playing in a natural context that is culturally and ecologically familiar. Children appear to have an exploratory drive to engage with the outdoor environment. In Chapter 2, it is suggested that as a species, we have a collective and cultural memory of play and learning through the natural environment, which is socially mediated through generational exchange and guided participation. Elemental play draws upon a triadic process between child and environment and adult, with the environment being the interconnecting factor. Humans have evolved due to their exploration, dexterity, imagination, problem-solving and community activities and we see consistent behaviour in very young children. Many children form profound and long-standing attachments to a local place or places where imaginary, tactile and physical experiences have occurred on a regular guided and self-chosen basis; many of these places have a generational and familial history. Chawla (1994: 165–6) records:

> those who model care, whether they be male or female, tend to perceive nature as an ordered, resourceful ally. My own research and experience confirm these observations. I have heard different combinations of these three forms of connection [child-watching, redoing time, and models of care] echoed by both men and women among conservationists who work to preserve places that they love, and by farmers with deep affection for their land. These people almost invariably tell me about an adult who bound them to nature as a child. These respondents also often express a sense of connection to the past and future generations – sometimes, in the men's cases, illustrated by their own accounts of child watching. Those who are farmers talk about the satisfactions of seasonal tasks. Informally, among men and women friends who practice a craft, I have heard the same connections when they discuss their commitment to reviving old techniques of work with natural materials.

Place, it has been argued, is important in the formation of self-identity. Elemental play provides a lens through which to see a spiritual dimension of children's development where vivid experiences of awe and wonder and being in one's element can be observed in children revelling in both the minute and the grand.

In Chapter 5, the four major elements are discussed as having a long history of cultural significance towards which children are naturally drawn. This elemental playfulness is an instinctive, human and cultural disposition and provides a further layer to Bronfenbrenner's ecological systems theory, explaining an individual's development and understanding of their place in the world around them. The everyday fascinations of nature and its diverse affordance for imaginative and creative play reflect ancient links with storytelling, myth, magic and mysteries. Children seem more able to pursue their own creative learning journeys in an outdoor environment that contains open-ended and playful possibilities. Loose, natural materials afford the possibility for a child to embark upon and prolong repeated activity, skill development and problem-solving as their internal ideas become externalised in autonomous projects.

Loose materials

It is the Loose Parts Theory of Nicholson (1971) and how his ideas have permeated the design and construction of many outdoor environments in the last thirty years or so that now appear so familiar to landscape architects working within early years. He wrote: 'In any environment, both the degree of inventiveness and creativity, and the possibility of discovery, are directly proportional to the number and kinds of variables' (p. 30). This idea seems to echo a similar ideology of both the pioneers who began to think about and provide specific environments for young children and the psychologists who developed theories of how children learn. Broadhead and Burt (2012: 31) confirm that:

> Loose Parts Theory advocates the value of open-ended play materials to accord with the ideas and possibilities that develop in children's minds as they play. Nicholson observed the building of children's playgrounds in the 1960s and commented that, whereas children played there when they were under construction, they ceased to do so once they were complete; there was no longer any challenge or interest in the adult-themed pre-determined spaces they had become. Brown (2003: 56–57) [states] 'flexibility in the play environment leads to increased flexibility in the child. The child is then better able to make use of the flexible environment . . . and moves closer to their developmental potential than would otherwise have been the case'.

The description of playgrounds under construction resonates with the Adventure Playground movement started by Sørenson in Copenhagen during World War Two:

> Originally known as junk playgrounds, these projects were conceived as spaces where city children, could, with waste material, create spaces that reflected their own vision. [They] proliferated in early 1950s England as a way for the population to reclaim derelict urban spaces. These places allow children a rare sensory agency over their own environment.
> (Dunn and MacPhee, 2010: 107–12)

Having had a role as adventure playground leader in the mid-1970s, setting up a small urban playground on the site of a demolished warehouse and working with a parent cooperative, it was very clear to me that both children and the adults of the community were highly engaged in supporting this playground and it existed for some ten years before the space was reclaimed for housing. Children built their own shelters, used real tools and were in control of the environment they were constructing. The children demonstrated a maturity of thinking previously undiscovered by us as workers in the street play previously observed. Watts (2011: 2) concurs; she cites Tizard (1976) who 'noticed that in a free play situation, children would choose to spend 75% of their time outside. Their level of play was more complex and mature than when indoors.'

There was positive social interaction, teamwork, emerging skill mastery and imaginative use of whatever materials we could scrounge. It was a time when scrap stores were being set up. There are now websites and companies selling 'play pods' and 'scrap store play pods' for delivery to schools and centres, with containers delivered on site full of the kinds of materials listed below. They were older children, but I am reminded of a school once visited where, as Nicholson suggested, the three-year-old children were much more interested in the construction of a gravel path, and the transporting of the gravel once it was completed, than the fixed, plastic equipment now available for them to climb on.

In the previous chapter, it is noted that loose natural materials allow children to follow their own ideas and unique creative connections. A brief search of current authors who write about early years play outdoors reveals the current list of loose materials shown in Table 8.1 that can and should be available for children's play.

TABLE 8.1 Range of possible loose materials that afford autonomous play

Tyres	Edgington, 2002; Bilton, 2008; Garrick, 2011
Builders trays	Bilton, 2008; Broadhead and Burt, 2012
Tunnels	Garrick, 2011
Containers	Garrick, 2011; Broadhead and Burt, 2012
Wheelbarrows	Garrick, 2011
Tubes, spools, pipes, syphons	Edgington, 2002; Curtis and Carter, 2003; Maxwell et al., 2008; Broadhead and Burt, 2012
Gutters	Edgington, 2002; Curtis and Carter, 2003; Broadhead and Burt, 2012
Crates	Edgington, 2002; Curtis and Carter, 2003; Williams-Siegfredson, 2012
Pallets	Curtis and Carter, 2003
Planks	Curtis and Carter, 2003; Broadhead and Burt, 2012
Sawhorses	Curtis and Carter, 2003
Poles and pulleys	Curtis and Carter, 2003
Clothes lines, rope	Edgington, 2002; Curtis and Carter, 2003
Real tools, inc. shovels, rakes, brushes, brooms, saws, hammers, sifters, trowels, measure tapes	Edgington, 2002; Curtis and Carter, 2003
Spray bottles, hoses, sprinklers, rain gauges	Curtis and Carter, 2003
Ramps	Curtis and Carter, 2003
Bikes, go-carts	Maxwell et al., 2008; Williams-Siegfredson, 2012
Wooden clothes horses	Edgington, 2002; Broadhead and Burt, 2012
Ropes	Broadhead and Burt, 2012
Fabric	Elliott, presentation, 2010; Maxwell et al., 2008; Broadhead and Burt, 2012
Large blocks	Maxwell et al., 2008; Broadhead and Burt, 2012
Cardboard boxes	Edgington, 2002; Broadhead and Burt, 2012
Loose parts in general	Nicholson, 1971; Rivkin, 1995; Casey, 2007; Maxwell et al., 2008; Knight, 2009; Tovey, 2011

These are not *natural materials* but *found materials* that children enjoy using in connection with the landscape and environments they encounter. Elemental play encompasses the constructivity of children engaged with places and things, 'messy, awkward, funny, frustrating, breathtaking and always almost unpredictable' (Casey, 2007: 2). Greenman (1988: 29) cites Piaget (1974) who said: 'To understand is to discover, or reconstruct by discovering. (20) Every new truth to be learned [is to] be rediscovered or at least reconstructed by the student, and not simply imparted to him (15).' Greenman also cites Montessori (1967: 27) who argues at length:

> If you watch a child of 3, you will see that he is always playing with something. This means that he is working out, and making conscious, something that his unconscious mind had earlier absorbed. Through this outward experience, in the guise of a game, he examines those things and impressions that he has taken in unconsciously. He becomes fully conscious and constructs the future man, by means of his activities . . . he does it through his hands, by experience, first in play, then through work.

Bjorkland and Pellegrini (2002: 302–3) concur:

> Much time is spent exploring the environment rather than playing with it; it is an information gathering venture and is evidenced, in its earliest forms, by mouthing and simple manipulation of objects. Through exploration, children come to know their environments. This knowledge provides the basis for play; exploration must be considered separate from play. The value, or function, of exploration may be that it affords animals the opportunity to learn about the properties of their immediate environments and about new and different niches.

Natural resources

In Chapter 2, the encounter with James demonstrated how a child as young as one year old was able to connect something found (a blue shoe) with a natural mobile of cones and shells, alongside adults working within the community sited near a beach. This cache of loose materials afforded James' participation in a culturally mediated activity.

The building of dens and shelters with loose materials is also a prevalent activity for young children. Generally, outdoors, a collection of both found and natural resources supports a nesting behaviour. White and Woolley (2014: 31) discuss 'Appleton's Habitat Theory (1975) in which preferences for particular landscape features are seen to correspond with an evolutionary ancient and deep-seated psychological drive to ensure that our survival needs are met.' Heft and Chawla (2006: 204–5) cite Gibson's eco-psychology which 'places humans in a world in which they have co-evolved with other living things. This eco-perspective implies human beings' dependence on the intrinsic qualities of the world, its resources, and its limits.'

Den or bush-cubby making generally occurs outside, when natural space and resources are available, but given the opportunity and freedom to use materials to hand, it will happen indoors with cushions, boxes, duvets and beds. Outside, children seem naturally drawn to finding, and being guided to, building structures themselves, much as in the Adventure Playgrounds in the 1970s, and now as a common activity in forest schools. Kylin (2003: 21, cited in Elliott, 2008: 7) claims

TABLE 8.2 Access to a range of natural materials

Sand	Hay and Nye, 2006; Edgington, 2002; Bilton, 2008; Casey, 2007; Williams-Siegfredson, 2012
Gravel	Bilton, 2008
Water	Hay and Nye, 2006; Edgington, 2002; Bilton, 2008
Small pebbles	Edgington, 2002; Curtis and Carter, 2003; Bilton, 2008; Broadhead and Burt, 2012
Tall grasses	Garrick, 2011
Small trees and shrubs	Garrick, 2011
Twigs and branches	Curtis and Carter, 2003; Spencer and Blades, 2006; Garrick, 2011; Broadhead and Burt, 2012
Seedheads, conkers, acorns, cones	Edgington, 2002; Curtis and Carter, 2003; Garrick, 2011
Soil/mud	Greenman, 1988; Hay and Nye, 2006; Spencer and Blades, 2006; Williams-Siegfredson, 2012; Broadhead and Burt, 2012
Logs	Edgington, 2002; Watts, 2011
Rocks and stones	Day, 2007; Watts, 2011
Hanging baskets	Edgington, 2002
Crystals	Day, 2007
Flowers	Greenman, 1988
Composting	Elliott, 2008
Worm farms	Elliott, 2008
Animals	Elliott, 2008
Wooden house, toadstool table and stools	Garrick, 2011
Willow tunnel	Garrick, 2011
Wigwam	Garrick, 2011
Bark	Greenman, 1988; Edgington, 2002; Bilton, 2008; Garrick, 2011
Haybales	Curtis and Carter, 2003
Boulders	Curtis and Carter, 2003
Shells	Edgington, 2002
Tree stumps	Maxwell et al., 2008

'The common factor in the experience of the den as a social and secret place is the sense of control that children feel they have, both over the den as a physical space and over the other children who share the den.'

Children do create dens out of blocks, crates and boxes, but appear to enjoy the wilder, more natural loose materials we can provide, or those that can be found in copses, woodlands and forests. A further search of current authors (Table 8.2) reveals a consistent list of natural materials we can provide in outdoor environments.

Hart (1977, cited by Moore and Young, 1978: 120) recorded that children spent a large amount of time building places for themselves, and observed that many of the 'houses' of children under eight were 'found' places with scarcely any major physical modification. They nevertheless served the users well, who modified and differentiated their interiors via their imaginations rather than by hand. He concluded that a requirement of building activity was a 'flexible landscape' to ensure a ready supply of 'loose parts'. Cobb (1977/1993: 57), writing contemporaneously with Hart, suggests:

> Although his tools are cultural, the child's modelling impulses, perceptual and manual, appear to be spontaneous and biologically innate. The natural properties of an artefact – its shape, colour, and especially its texture and potential use – are the reality, along with the identity.

She further writes: 'Mankind is (and has been, since the emergence of Homo Sapiens) biologically the same, and man has always felt this need to know and to organize the world around him' (p. 97). There are links here with Chapters 3 and 7. Children need to develop their own ideas and projects, and follow these more evidently in spaces and with resources of their own choosing.

Provision of zones and areas of outdoor activity

The range of materials listed in Table 8.2 afford children autonomous space and place making within the found or provided environment. Many practitioners will be familiar with the notion of affordance, and it is an integral concept within elemental play:

> 'Affordance' is a central construct of ecological perceptual psychology. It is generally defined as the physical opportunities and dangers which the organism perceives while acting in a specific setting. Objects afford grasping, twisting, throwing, surfaces afford running, climbing etc. This concept has the potential to be extended to comprise emotional, social and cultural opportunities that the individual perceives in the environment and of the individual, it is located at the interface between the setting and the person (Gibson, 1979).
>
> (Kyttä, 2006: 141)

Space and place making has been an important inclusion in many authors' ideas. Titman (1994: 20) states that:

> Proshansky and Fabian (1987) describe place identity as the 'physical-world socialisation of the child'. They suggest that place identity is 'a substructure of the person's self-identity that is comprised of cognitions about the physical environment that also serve to define who the person is' . . . children look at the environment in terms of its physical and social meanings in order to understand their surroundings, to satisfy their needs and in so doing learn to behave appropriately. They believe that the ability to 'read' environments and to form concepts about place-identity is essential to a child's development of a sense of competence and control of the physical world, which is in turn an important aspect of self-identity.

Brown (in Wattchow and Brown, 2011: 16–17) cites Park (1995: 320) who is categorical: 'a sense of place is a fundamental human need'; Brown also comments on the

> importance of the social, cultural, historical and geographical dimensions of lived experience. We are who we are because of where we are and the experiences we have had. The meaning/s we give to events, possessions, places and people are bound to situation and context.

In Chapter 3, the discussion of attachment to place was presented as crucial to the concept of elemental play. Titman (1994: 84) cites Moore (1980) who 'found that the most dominant reason which children gave for liking particular places was to experience the natural environment, animal life, vegetation, weather and other sensory qualities.'

Invariably, landscape architects now follow Clark's (2010) 'mosaic approach' when initially considering any change or development to an outdoor environment. Young children often list 'secret' or 'hiding places' as desirable for their playful adventures. This is also reflected in authors' defined areas to provide in early years outdoor environments (Table 8.3).

Environmental principles

The rationale for including these varied areas for different play possibilities are often incorporated in a set of principles when authors are considering the types of environment we can provide for very young children. Ryder Richardson (2006) suggests five:

1. The special nature of outdoors and the freedom we associate with it.
2. Contact with the natural world and the space for whole-body, multi-sensory experiences.

TABLE 8.3 Designing and organising outdoor spaces

Creative	Bilton, 2008; Spencer and Blades, 2006
Imaginative, stories, music, reading	Edgington, 2002; Bilton, 2008; Watts, 2011
Open spaces	Bilton, 2008
Environmental area	Bilton, 2008
Wild area, tangled area, wild places	Edgington, 2002; Bilton, 2008; Elliott, 2008; Garrick, 2011; Tovey, 2013
Digging area, mud patches	Edgington, 2002; Bilton, 2008; Elliott, 2008; Williams-Siegfredson, 2012
Growing area	Edgington, 2002; Bilton, 2008; Watts, 2011; Tovey, 2013
Gymnastic area, climbing	Edgington, 2002; Bilton, 2008; Day, 2007; Tovey, 2011
Pond, water courses, splash areas, fountains	Edgington, 2002; Kahn and Kellert, 2002; Casey, 2007; Elliott, 2008; Watts, 2011
Screens	Casey, 2007; Knight, 2009
High lookout	Casey, 2007
Courtyard	Casey, 2007
Auditorium	Casey, 2007
Stage, performance area, meeting space	Casey, 2007; Garrick, 2011
Sandpit	Edgington, 2002; Elliott, 2008; Maxwell et al., 2008; Williams-Siegfredson, 2012
Cozy backyard	Curtis and Carter, 2003
Large planting	Curtis and Carter, 2003
Secret places, special places	Edgington, 2002; Kahn and Kellert, 2002; Spencer and Blades, 2006; Elliott, 2008; Tovey, 2013
Cubbies/dens	Elliott, 2008
Firepit	Day, 2007; Knight, 2009; Williams-Siegfredson, 2012
Building	Day, 2007
'The whatever you want it to be place'	Broadhead and Burt, 2012

3. Authentic and dynamic experience of space, place and perspective.
4. The opportunity for challenge and managing safety.
5. The different relationships encountered with adults and children.

Curtis and Carter (2003: 14–18), writing in America, have a broader set of principles to take into account when transforming early childhood environments:

1. Creating connections and a sense of belonging.
2. Keeping space flexible and materials open-ended.

3. Designing a natural environment that engage our senses.
4. Provoking wonder, curiosity and intellectual engagement.
5. Engaging in symbolic representation, literacy and the visual arts.

Kimes Myers (1997) in earlier research (Myers and Myers, 1992: 63) considers four core conditions in a spirituality of caring in relation to environmental provision:

1. The provision of hospitable space.
2. The acceptance, embracing, and providing of experiences.
3. The presence of authentic, caring adults.
4. An affirmation of the process of learning ... of being able to spiritedly transcend present conditions.

Elliott (2008: 5) has researched and developed environmental and child-friendly play spaces in Australia; she writes about an outdoor playspace as:

1. Reflecting local landscape and climate.
2. Dominated by natural elements.
3. Invites open-ended interaction, exploration and manipulation.
4. Provides opportunities for risk-taking, spontaneity and discovery.
5. Stimulates all the senses.
6. Alive and unique.
7. Accessible at all times and in all weathers.
8. Promotes a sense of place for children and adults.
9. Contains multiple habitats.
10. Promotes a sense of wonder.
11. Is always evolving and never finished.

Hocking (2008: 136) describes four layers of complexity:

1. The playspace as a whole and its dynamic backdrop for children's play.
2. Defined smaller areas to act as foci for specific dramatic and creative experiences.
3. Loose materials and equipment.
4. The prevailing and seasonal weather conditions.

If the provision of 1, 2 and 4 is sound, she argues, the less daily effort is required by adults to shift heavy and semi-fixed equipment and the more the children will own their play, moving their own loose parts and using the prevailing conditions they encounter on a daily basis.

As early as 1995, Rivkin set guidelines for planning playgrounds; she suggests

1. Take an inventory.
2. Clarify goals for children.
3. Analyse the available space and zoning the playground – more play spaces lead to diverse activity.
4. Provide loose parts.
5. Consider local climate and weather.
6. Make activities and equipment accessible.
7. Ensure children and staff are involved in planning.

White and Woolley (2014: 30) give a contemporary update and list six concepts that characterise a good outdoor environment for children:

1. Physically diverse.
2. Generous – for enquiry, discovery and thinking.
3. Supportive – for feeling nurtured, calm and imaginative.
4. Secure – for feeling comfortable and at home.
5. Agency – for being in control and feeling powerful.
6. For travelling, journeying and adventure.

Wilson (2012: 21) who bases these principles on Ceppi and Zini (1998), Greenman (2005) and Wellhousen (2002), also considers the holistic development of children, and which can be applied equally to indoor environments and outdoor spaces:

1. Experience new physical challenges.
2. Develop strength and stamina.
3. Use large muscles and fine muscles in new ways.
4. Engage in problem-solving.
5. Interact with peers by talking and playing.
6. Appreciate nature and protect the environment.
7. Express abilities and curiosity.
8. Explore and research alone, and with other (both peers and adults).
9. Reinforce a sense of autonomy and security.
10. Experience beauty, comfort, sensory stimulation, excitement, wonder, and joy.

White (2014) later adds that key experiences should include sensing and making sense of the world, developing vision and hearing, providing opportunity for sleeping, moving in space and gravity, exploring natural elements, making things happen and being together with adults. Heft and Chawla (2006: 206) suggest four additional conditions that support the development of children's environmental competencies:

1. Affordances that promote discovery and responsive person-environment relationships.
2. Access and mobility to engage affordances.
3. Guided participation that supports perceptual learning and action.
4. Opportunities for meaningful participation in community settings.

These are similar to Derr's (2006: 119) ideas of freedom, control and self-sufficiency that appear to be afforded when playing outside. In special places, she argues, children experience greater opportunities for creativity, imagination and getting away from others to centre oneself. In addition, children can learn care and develop a sense of responsibility, and respect and empathy towards other living things. These dispositions will then support the development of a child's identity and may help form attachments to place.

Zini (2006: 29, cited in Casey, 2007: 7) concurs: 'if a child's identity is formed through a complex and fascinating alchemy of environmental adventures and genetic history, then the wider the range of environmental experience on offer, the more opportunities there are for supporting each child's developmental journey'. We are minded here of earlier chapters where children are seen to identify with natural places and spaces characterised by particular fantastic and imaginary experiences: Waller's (2007) trampoline tree, Mills' (n.d.) goblin cave and the magic chocolate pit. All three involved children becoming secure in their own identity as adventurers and storytellers:

> a way of being baptized into the world by immersion, such as children in play who literally live close to the ground and up against the full sensory quality of things – making hiding places under table and bushes, climbing trees, rolling down hills, squatting in the mud and water, and peering under rocks, surrounded by smell, textures and details that the adult height and habits will later remove from them.
>
> (Chawla, 2002: 209)

White and Woolley (2014: 37) cite Tovey (2007), who agrees:

> The outdoor environment for young children is a dynamic, living place . . . it is a domain that takes shape as children, or children and adults inhabit it. Children interact with the environment almost like a play partner, shaping and transforming it, but in turn being shaped by the experiences and interactions it enables . . . Children, then, should be 'authors', as well as 'readers' of their environments.

Forest schools and gardens

With authority, Knight (2009, 2011) writes about forest schools and affirms that:

1. Setting is not the usual one.
2. Is made as safe as is reasonably possible in order to facilitate children's risk-taking.
3. Happens over time.
4. There is no such thing as bad weather, only bad clothing.
5. Trust is central.
6. The learning is play-based and, as far as possible, child-initiated and child-led.
7. The blocks and sessions have beginning and ends.
8. The staff are trained.

(2009: 15)

Over the last ten years, there has been a surge of interest in forest schools, availability of training and exchange visits to Scandinavia to explore well-established forest kindergartens, nature kindergartens, wildlife groups and outdoor

---

ENCOUNTER: In the Millennium Wood

The forest school based in a small wood where children visited weekly from their preschool was darker in the summer because of the tree canopy; the canopy would act as a cloak against rain and we often brought head torches for the children to use, particular when they made dens in the rain. At other times in the summer, the grasses and nettles grew over head height, and the boundary journeys became jungle-like, the children completely disappearing in the green. During the late autumn, as more natural light got through, the rain would soak the ground level and at times the children would create mud cities, or ditches to be bridged by logs and branches. In the depth of winter, we would walk to the gate and take the public footpath adjacent to the field. Ploughed furrows would be full of ice to look at, smash, hold pieces of . . . and then it was off to the 'troll bridge' at the bottom of the field. And then, of course, in the spring, up would come the bluebells with the celandines and the robins gathered to welcome us back. The children created the identity and play in the wood very much in tune with the seasons and environmental conditions, returning to the 'lying tree' – a small tree, easily climbable and shaped to be able to lie in, knowing where cones could be collected, which plants harboured ladybirds and where the rabbit pellets would be. It was *their* forest school.

nurseries. Williams-Siegfredsen (2012: 9–10) considers the pedagogical theories that have informed present-day practice in Denmark, referring to Rousseau, Pestalozzi, Froebel, Dewey, Montessori, Piaget, Vygotsky, Goleman, Gardner and Csíkszentmihályi, summing up their influence as an:

1. Holistic approach to children's learning and development.
2. Each child as unique and competent.
3. Children are active and interactive learners.
4. Children need real-life, first-hand experiences.
5. Children thrive in child-centred environments.
6. Children need time to experiment and develop individual thinking.
7. Learning comes from social interactions.

Current and small-scale research at Little Muddy Boots in September 2015 evidenced the ongoing influence of Froebel and Pestalozzi, as the site is based in a large garden rather than a forest school or purpose-built environment.

Casey (2007: 9) cites Hart (1997: 18) who agrees that:

> We should feed children's natural desire to contact nature's diversity with free access to an area of limited size over an extended period of time for it is only by intimately knowing the wonders of nature's complexity in a particular place that one can fully appreciate the immense beauty of the planet as a whole.

It does feel important to introduce and sustain children's experiences of the cycles of life, to talk about and encounter solar cycles, seasonal cycles, nutrient and food cycles, the growing and water cycles, and to meet the life cycle in the emergence of larvae and butterflies, chicks from eggs and occasionally a blackbird who lies silent and cold at the base of a tree. We may then nurture the naturalist intelligence which Gardner (2006) identified in 2003. A child with:

1. Keen sensory skills.
2. Uses heightened sensory skills to notice and categorise things from the natural world.
3. Likes to be outside, or like activities like gardening, nature walks, or field trips geared towards observing nature or natural phenomena.
4. Easily notices patterns from surroundings – likes differences, similarities, anomalies.
5. Notices things in the environment others often miss.
6. Creates, keeps or has collections, scrapbooks, logs or journals about natural objects including notes, photos, drawings and specimens.
7. Interested in [vicarious] encounters – film, television, books and objects about nature, science or animals.

8. Heightened awareness/concern for the environment and/or endangered species.
9. Easily learns characteristics, names, categorisations and data about objects/species in natural world.

The leader of Little Muddy Boots, Hannah, has established a parent and toddler garden group, where leader and parents are engaged in mutual activities to encourage children to explore and learn outdoors and in all weathers with occasional visits to ponds and orchards to extend their growing understanding of wildlife, and the cycle of fruit and vegetable life. Each group of children (Tuesday, Thursday and Friday [2]) has their own 'patch' and there is a respect for each other's patch.

In asking the parents, Hannah, and Jess from the millennium wood forest school 'What did you hope the children would experience?' and 'Can you describe any "unlooked for experiences that you enjoyed?"', their answers included:

- I hoped that they would develop an interest in nature, an enjoyment of playing outdoors and that families would notice this and spend more time outside. I wanted the children to take exercise, increase their resilience, have lots of fun and benefit from the opportunity to play with friends and see through their own ideas with limited interruption yet ample adult support.
- Finding tadpoles in the stream we visit and being able to paddle alongside them and return to them each week. Visiting a muddy puddle whilst heading out for the walk and still being there watching the children play an hour later. Experiencing the recent solar eclipse; a handful of parents stayed and we felt the woods go cold.
- For them to get excited about growing their own vegetables and be intrigued about some of the wildlife that's on our doorstep.
- The club has been more than about gardening and is generally about the outdoor experience – looking for bugs, pond life, rainbows and sticks.
- Free play in amongst trees and dead leaves with other children.
- Planting and harvesting, making mud pies, learning about frogs, pond-dipping, clouds. Every week is an adventure.
- Extra activities such as a hedgehog visiting and a trip to the pond.
- Mud pies and water play. We talk about it all the time.
- Enjoying time outside interacting with plants and nature and learning basic gardening and outdoor skills in a friendly and welcoming environment with other children.

Elemental play with people, places and things; garden patch collectivity and wonder at the life cycles of plants and vegetables, where children pick and eat raw beans; the surprise visit of a hedgehog and tadpoles turning into frogs; rainbows and solar eclipse that are beyond the everyday, but are mysterious experiences connecting children to earthly occurrences.

On the day to day, most parents at Little Muddy Boots state that the children's favourite activity is the mud kitchen, to which they return week after week as their first journey in the garden. Hannah says 'I have been bowled over by the popularity (and continuing popularity) of the mud kitchen. Almost all the children *migrate* to it first and can sometimes be reluctant to leave.' It is not a big garden but Hannah has considered the space and features to include the mud kitchen adjacent to a very large water butt, where children have developed their skill to turn it on and off. There is a 'sound' fence where pots and pans hang and a water fence where pipes, tubes and funnels are attached; nearby a number of watering cans are available to be filled (and emptied) into the tubes to water the garden or to add to the mud kitchen. There are a number of small, contained garden patches and a series of tree stumps to sit on. Under a marquee are a number of creative resources and laminated sheets for leaf, tree and bug identification. Trowels and buckets are stored at ground level and there are small pots to use. There is a chalking board, grow bags, compost area, pole wigwams for climbing plants, some chairs and tables for 'café play' and a collection of immature trees at one end of the garden. Hannah has said:

> For some [children], the freedom of a garden to play in (a few have no garden or limited access to space that is theirs). For others, it's the chance to do what they love more often and explore further digging, planting and finding bugs, etc. Next year, I'm hoping to expand – with more sessions for children in more built up areas, where gardens are typically small, and sessions at local nurseries who have no/limited outdoor space, and finally with hopefully an assistant!

The garden is mostly grass, with many pathways created by the children's boots. It is fenced on three sides with solid wood, but the fencing acts as a frame to activities. There is compost and mud for growing, with a small copse at the fourth side where branches, undergrowth and leaves offer different textures. Bjorkland and Pellegrini (2002: 62–3) state that 'the garden is the essence of a Froebelian early years setting' and further,

> Direct experience of nature was essential to Froebel. Children learnt *in* nature rather than just *about* nature. Through gardening and play outdoors children were immersed in the natural world and could learn about the growth of plants and animals, about the beauty of nature and about the interrelationships of all living things. They also learnt to care for and take responsibility for nature and gradually to develop a sense of personal responsibility. Through gardening, children experience the cycles of life and depth, growth and decay, recycling and conserving resources in direct and meaningful ways. If children can develop a sense of wonder about nature, can see the effect of their ac-tions on things around them and can get to know their own small garden in deep ways, they are much more likely to want to help shape a sustainable future.

Outdoor surfaces

The garden described is an area that could be offered in many preschools, nurseries and schools where space is limited. Many landscape architects and authors imply that the space needed for outdoor provision is quite large, particularly when they list the range of surfaces that are ideal for exploratory, 'brave' and 'adventurous' play (McMillan, 1930). Many of the surfaces listed in Table 8.4 *will* afford vestibular and conceptual experiences so children experience first-hand, gradient, speed, distance, height and momentum. Many of us will have visited larger children's centres and schools in the UK and wider afield that have received funding to redesign exceptional landscapes for children which may include a few or many of the items in Table 8.4.

One is to feel encouraged, however, by the small-scale scope of the garden provided by Little Muddy Boots for very young children as it should present some ideas for practitioners with small or shared spaces.

Perceived challenges

There are recognisable challenges for staff in many early years settings to provide continuous provision (outdoor–indoor) for young children. Casey (2007: 13, 24) urges us to 'build a picture of the play, seek children's views, understand the space – the seasons and weather, physical features, light, the people and the setting'.

TABLE 8.4 Surfaces

Slopes, hillocks, grassy banks, mounds, uneven ground	Casey, 2007; Garrick, 2011; Watts, 2011; Tovey, 2011, 2013
Hollows	Casey, 2007
Corners	Watts, 2011
Soft matting	Garrick, 2011
Pathways, grass/herb pathway, winding tracks	Garrick, 2011
Bark chippings	Bilton, 2008
Slabs	Garrick, 2011
Stepping stones	Garrick, Curtis and Carter, 2003; Watts, 2011
Tunnels	Garrick, 2011; Tovey, 2011
Ditches	Tovey, 2011, 2013
Soft earth	Spencer and Blades, 2006
Boulders	Casey, 2007
Small pebbles, gravel	Bilton, 2008
Uneven ground	Watts, 2011; Tovey, 2013

Further 'to be inclusive, flexible, to offer shelter, centres of interest, natural features, sensory elements and atmosphere' (pp. 34–7); we can add, the opportunity for fresh air, materials that enable children to follow their own interests and time to watch and wait. In recent research (Woods, 2016), it was interesting accompanying a landscape architect to a small preschool to look at the levels of involvement of children and how they were using the space they had outside a church hall, in order to plan for possible changes to the environment (see Chapter 5). There was little that could be changed regarding the levels or the surfaces, but the range of equipment provided, apart from the sand kitchen was not particularly holding the children's attention. When a practitioner brought some water and brushes outside, the levels of involvement increased. Simple changes could be made:

- The storage shed was crammed full of bikes, scooters, plastic garages; some were broken, and all had to be put away at the end of each session. Tools, buckets, large brushes, some wheeled trucks, wheelbarrows, extension play to the mud kitchen would be easier to store and be more open-ended. With agreement from the church committee, stores of large pebbles, logs, tree trunk discs and stumps, cones, branches and sticks could be stored outside for natural weathering and loose parts play.
- Head torches, magnifying glasses, torches, fabric, a couple of clothes horses would also take up a smaller space and perhaps less likely to be provided in a home environment where bikes, trikes and scooters are more usually the norm.
- Asking for a water supply or a couple of rain barrels outside would afford the possibility of pouring and mixing, painting, extensive mud/sand kitchen activity, gutter/pipe and crate play.
- A large tyre could provide sandpit space or growing space for some vegetables or flowers.
- Wellington boots and outdoor clothing may also be stored outside in the shed for children to access.

This group did have continuous provision; the children could go in and out as they chose. It is acknowledged that this may be a difficulty for many practitioners but it is crucial to really get underneath a perceived problem and work out whether it is space, entrance/exit, storage, reluctance to be outside on behalf of the adult but also to explore any reluctance, perceived risks, ratio of staff to children or fixed equipment that has been provided and takes up all the space. We can change the surfaces outside to more natural ones, provide growing boxes and hanging baskets, screen off areas and change chairs to tree stumps. We can also remove slides and bring in logs to climb and sit on. Tree stumps can be rolled and crates can be stacked for use and come to no harm outside. Wooden fences can have pipes and tubes attached as well as sound makers; mesh fencing can be used for weaving. Fences can also be used to attach tarpaulin and fabric to, and provide cosy shelters and shade for quieter play. Ideally:

> A playground should be like a small scale replica of the world, with as many as possible of the sensory experiences found in the world included in it. Experience of every sense are needed: rough and smooth objects to look at and feel; light and heavy things to pick up; water and wet materials, as well as dry things; cool materials and material warmed by the sun; soft and hard surfaces; things that make sounds like running water, or that can be struck, plucked and plinked; smells of all varieties; shiny, bright objects and dull, dark ones, things both huge and tiny; high and low places to look at and from; mats of every type: natural, synthetic, thin, thick and so on. The list is inexhaustible, and the larger the number of objects that are included, the richer and more varied the environment for the child.
>
> (Dattner, 1969: 44, cited in Greenman, 1988: 177)

It can also be argued, the richer and more varied the play will be, because of the multi-purposeness of the materials. Once again, we can revisit the concepts introduced in previous chapters; elemental play involves the dynamic and investigative relationship between people, places and things that reflect both the elements and the elemental forces surrounding the child.

Indoor provision

Not all of these natural materials need to be outside. I only thought the other day that having introduced my four-month-old granddaughter to a dried hydrangea flower in the garden which she delighted in grasping and crunching in her little hand, I ought to bring some inside for her to further explore. May et al. (2006: 9–10) claim that 'if the practitioner finds interesting, stimulating and curious things in the setting, then the children will as well'. In the previous chapter, Ryder explains her rationale for 'throwing out the plastic' after a particularly interesting observation of play with pebbles outside, and following a visit to Reggio Emilia. Boyd Cadwell (1997: 5, 22) recalls:

> the educators in Reggio Emilia view *the environment as a third teacher*. The design and use of space encourage encounters, communication and relationships (Gandini, 1993). There is an underlying order and beauty in the design and organization of all the space in a school and the equipment and materials within it (Lewin, 1995).
>
> The pigments of paint, the mixture of yarns, the weight and wetness of clay come from the earth. They are the earth. We often use these materials to make connections, to build bridges, to create our own renderings and responses to what we experience in the world. We play with them as we play with stones, or shells on the beach to create our own arrangements, to make our own beauty, to reach out to the natural world and participate in it. We do not do this in isolation. We do it most often in the company of friends or for a wider audience. We invite response to what we do, whether we do it alone, in pairs, or in a

TABLE 8.5 Bringing the outdoors in

Sand tray with plastic toys	Sand within tarpaulin on the floor; sleepers to envelop edges of tarpaulin.
	Coir compost, earth, gravel, shavings, autumn leaves.
	Add shells, cones, small woven baskets, sticks, pebbles, plant and herb cuttings.
Water tray with plastic toys	Natural sponges, pond weed, goldfish,* shells, stones, pebbles, sticks, seaweed, cork.
	Sand and water trays can be adjacent for mixing.
Home corner/ imaginary play	Teepee with boughs from outside; bamboo fence panels for screens.
Small-world play with blocks, plastic bricks, animals and figures	Logs, branches, moss, leaves, tree stumps, rocks, pebbles, rope, hessian.
Display	Plants for flowers and/or herbs, feathers, nests, rocks, shells, crystals, torches, light box, prisms, fossils, conch shells, willow weavings; stick insects, chick incubator, a wormery, caterpillar/butterfly farm.
Memory games with pictures and plastic objects	Natural resources, feely bags, sounds of birds and animals.
Mathematical activities with plastic objects	Different length sticks for measuring; cones, shells, pebbles for weighing.
Treasure baskets	Loofahs, sponges, brushes, feathers, citrus fruit, cones, pebbles, shells, soft leather.

Note: *Goldfish: what a delight for children to see a fish or two swimming about! Suggest a second tray so that children still have the opportunity for water play.

group. We want to know if what we make, what we say, what we write, what we shape, makes sense, communicates, tells the story we had in mind.

Nature inspires beauty; play with natural materials demonstrates higher levels of involvement and well-being (Davey, 2013; Woods, 2016). Children seem to have a greater respect for nature and natural resources when they can handle and experience them authentically. Indoors, our equipment and furniture is largely wood and plastic, both smooth and hard materials. We do have fabrics for dressing up and recycled objects for collage and junk modelling. We perhaps need to think about the variety of textures outside and the range of *forces*, combinations and play children enact and experience. In Table 8.5, suggestions, not an exhaustive list, are given for increasing the range of natural materials inside.

Many resources can be recycled and refreshed without great cost, and *more of less* materials works well – pebbles, shells, crates, pipes, sand – because they afford such a diverse range of playful ideas: 'It seems reasonable to conclude that experience of the natural environment is one of the crucial continuities in human life, giving adults a recollected "grounding" in their childhood years' (Moore and Young, 1978: 111).

When carrying out small-scale research with the forest school (2015), I asked the leader, Jess: 'To what extent have you noticed in the levels of outdoor play/interest in natural resources (including weather) changed during sessions in pre-school and, secondly, in what ways might have the sessions in the wood made you re-evaluate outdoor play?' Her responses should give some confidence to practitioners who would like to alter the balance of in/outdoor activities and resources:

> There was already free flow between the outdoors and the indoors for much of the session at preschool, but other staff are now less likely to keep children inside during spells of heavy rain. We have developed a mud kitchen, and increased natural resources (e.g. logs, pebbles, etc.) but if I can find the time I think that there is a lot more I/we could do to bring the best of forest school back to the village hall setting. The whole team support forest school and see that children can learn as much outside as in. Maybe historically outside was seen as a place just to go and have a runabout and let off steam. It has made me question how open-ended the resources are which we put out and to increase the proportion of the day, particularly in the summer, when the children can be outside. It also made me notice how much more effort, in terms of staff allocation, is put into setting up inside rather than outside.

This thought is similar to the research and practice carried out by Burt (Broadhead and Burt, 2012), who found that once staff had re-organised space outside to be the 'whatever you want it to be space', they began to question the time spent on planning minutely for learning activities *inside* the classroom and began to change their overall pedagogical approach to reflect a more natural and playful domain, as had been achieved outside.

Day (2007: 172) concludes:

> Nature refreshes the soul. In hectic, hard-edged, traffic-dominated environments, eyes crave greenery and leaf shade for relief. To Olds (2001) trees, gardens, animals, water and views provide many physically and emotionally healing benefits, in addition to enhancing a child's knowledge of the natural world. Indeed if we are to save this planet, exposing children to the wonders of nature at a very young age is essential.

This exposure, as suggested by the notion of elemental play, is culturally and historically grounded in our evolution and seems vital to the continued sustainability and invention of human society. In the next chapter, the recognition of play as a fundamental activity of childhood is explored.

Provocations

- Elemental play is an action and encounter with the world; it values learning through the presented environment. Given the suggestions in the chapter, in which area could you present more natural materials?
- Look outside. Consider the floor surfaces, boundaries, and fixed equipment in relation to diversity of tactile, sensory, visual and physical experiences. What could you do to change one thing, and how would you go about it?
- Where do children explore in your setting?
- If our settings are to become places of encounter, where do we offer children the opportunity to experiment, innovate and research?
- There may be limitations to the space and opportunity you have for outdoor play. Where could you go in your local environment to allow for exploration and diversity of natural encounters?
- A suggestion of throwing out the plastic has been made; what is your reaction and how might you increase the range of natural materials indoors?
- Debbie Ryder is researching parents' and teachers' perceptions as to what physical activity experiences are happening in the early years and homes settings. Her hypothesis is that due to a possible lack of discussion and understanding between the home and early years setting, parents may be thinking physical activity occurs in the early years setting while teachers may be thinking it occurs at home. Reflect on this hypothesis and what you know about the physical encounters children experience both in and away from your setting.

References

Bilton, H. (ed.) (2008) *Learning Outdoors. Improving the Quality of Young Children's Play Outdoors*. London: David Fulton.

Bjorkland, D.F. and Pellegrini, A.D. (2002) *The Origins of Human Nature: Evolutionary Developmental Psychology*. Washington, DC: American Psychological Association.

Boyd Cadwell, L. (1997) *Bringing Reggio Emilia Home: An Innovative Approach to Early Childhood Education*. New York: Teachers College Press.

Broadhead, P. and Burt, A. (2012) *Understanding Young Children's Learning through Play: Building Playful Pedagogies*. London: Routledge.

Casey, T. (2007) *Environments for Outdoor Play. A Practical Guide to Making Space for Children*. London: PCP.

Chawla, L. (1994) *In the First Country of Places, Nature, Poetry, and Childhood Memory*. New York: State University of New York Press.

Chawla, L. (2002) Spots of time: manifold ways of being in nature in childhood. In P.H. Kahn, Jr. and S.R. Kellert (eds) *Children and Nature. Psychological, Sociocultural and Evolutionary Investigations.* Cambridge, MA: MIT Press, pp. 199–226.

Clark, A. (2010) *Transforming Children's Spaces:. Children's and Adults' Participation in Designing Learning Environments.* London: Routledge.

Cobb, E. (1977/1993) *The Ecology of Imagination in Childhood.* Connecticut: Spring Publications.

Curtis, D. and Carter, M. (2003) *Designs for Living and Learning. Transforming Early Childhood Environments.* St Paul, MN: Redleaf Press.

Davy, A. (2013) Using Leuven observation and assessment tools to investigate outdoor provision. In J. Georgeson and J. Payler (eds) *International Perspectives on Early Childhood Education and Care.* Maidenhead: Open University Press, pp. 216–28.

Day, C. (2007) *Environment and Children: Passive Lessons from the Everyday Environment.* Oxford: Architectural Press.

Derr, T. (2006) 'Sometimes birds sound like fish': perspectives on children's place experiences. In C. Spencer and M. Blades (eds) *Children and their Environments: Learning, Using and Designing Spaces.* Cambridge: Cambridge University Press, pp. 108–23.

Dunn, A. and MacPhee, J. (eds) (2010) *SIGNAL: 01 Adventure Playgrounds.* Oakland, CA: PM Press.

Edgington, M. (2002) *The Great Outdoors. Developing Children's Learning through Outdoor Provision.* London: British Association for Early Childhood Education.

Elliott, S. (ed.) (2008) *The Outdoor Playspace Naturally for Children Birth to Five Years.* Castle Hill, NSW, Australia: Pademelon Press.

Gardner, H. (2006) *The Development and Education of the Mind. The Selected Works of Howard Gardner.* London and New York: Routledge.

Garrick, R. (2011) A responsive environment: creating a dynamic, versatile and flexible environment. In J. White (ed.) *Outdoor Provision in the Early Years.* London: Sage, pp. 45–56.

Greenman, J. (1988) *Caring Spaces, Learning Places: Children's Environments That Work.* Redmond, WA: Exchange Press.

Hay, D. with Nye, R. (2006) *The Spirit of the Child*, rev. edn. London: Jessica Kingsley.

Heft, H. and Chawla, L. (2006) Children as agents in sustainable development: the ecology of competence. In C. Spencer and M. Blades (eds) *Children and their Environments. Learning, Using and Designing Spaces.* Cambridge: Cambridge University Press, pp. 199–216.

Hocking, M. (2008) Planning for children in natural playspaces. In S. Elliott (ed.) The Outdoor Playspace Naturally for Children Birth to Five Years. Castle Hill, NSW, Australia: Pademelon Press, pp. 133–52.

Kahn, Jr. P.H. and Kellert, S.R. (eds) (2002) *Children and Nature. Psychological, Sociocultural and Evolutionary Investigations.* Cambridge, MA: MIT Press.

Kimes Myers, B. (1997) *Young Children and Spirituality.* London: Routledge.

Knight, S. (2009) *Forest Schools and Outdoor Learning in the Early Years*. London: Sage.

Knight, S. (2011) *Risk and Adventure in Early Years Outdoor Play. Learning from Forest Schools*. London: Sage.

Kyttä, M. (2006) Environmental child-friendliness in the light of the Bullerby Model. In C. Spencer and M. Blades (eds) *Children and their Environments: Learning, Using and Designing Spaces*. Cambridge: Cambridge University Press, pp. 141–60.

Louv, R. (2012) *The Nature Principle: Reconnecting with Life in a Virtual Age*. Chapel Hill, NC: Algonquin.

Maxwell, L.E., Mitchell, M.R. and Evans, G.W. (2008) Effects of play equipment and loose parts on preschool children's outdoor play behaviour: an observational study and design intervention. *Children, Youth and Environments* 18(2): 37–63.

May, P. Ashford, E. and Bottle, G. (2006) *Sound Beginnings: Learning and Development in the Early Years*. London: David Fulton.

McMillan, M. (1930) *The Nursery School*. London and Toronto: J. M. Dent & Sons.

Mills, J. (n.d.) Children's relationships with outdoor spaces. Unpublished.

Moore, R. and Young, D. (1978) Childhood outdoors: toward a social ecology of the landscape. In I. Altman and J.F. Wohlwill (eds) *Human Behaviour and Environment, Advances in Theory and Research. Vol. 3: Children and the Environment*. New York: Plenum Press, pp. 83–30.

Nicholson, S. (1971) How NOT to cheat children: the theory of loose parts. *Landscape Architecture* 62: 30–4.

Rivkin, M.S. (1995) *The Great Outdoors. Restoring Children's Right to Play Outside*. Washington, DC: National Association for the Education of Young Children.

Ryder Richardson, G. (2006) *Creating a Space to Grow: Developing Your Outdoor Learning Environment*. London: David Fulton.

Spencer, C. and Blades, M. (eds) *Children and their Environments: Learning, Using and Designing Spaces*. Cambridge: Cambridge University Press.

Titman, W. (1994) Special places; special people. The hidden curriculum of school grounds. http://files.eric.ed.gov/fulltext/ED430384.pdf (accessed 14 April 2003).

Tovey, H. (2011) Achieving the balance: challenge, risk and safety. In J. White (ed.) *Outdoor Provision in the Early Years*. London: Sage, pp. 86–94.

Tovey, H. (2013) *Bringing the Froebel Approach to your Early Years Practice*. London: David Fulton.

Waller, T. (2007) 'The trampoline tree and the swamp monster with 18 heads': outdoor play in the foundation stage and foundation phase. *Education 3–13*, 35(4): 393–407.

Wattchow, B. and Brown, M. (2011) *A Pedagogy of Place. Outdoor Education for a Changing World*. Clayton, Vic., Australia: Monash University.

Watts, A. (2011) *Every Nursery Needs a Garden: A Step-by-Step Guide to Creating and Using a Garden with Young Children*. London: David Fulton.

White, J. (2014) Exploring appropriate outdoor provision for babies and toddlers. In T. Maynard and J. Waters (eds) *Exploring Outdoor Play in the Early Years*. Maidenhead: Open University Press, pp. 42–54.

White, J. and Woolley, H. (2014) What makes a good outdoor environment for young children? In T. Maynard and J. Waters (eds) *Exploring Outdoor Play in the Early Years*. Maidenhead: Open University Press, pp. 29–41.

Williams-Siegfredsen, J. (2012) *Understanding the Danish Forest School Approach: Early Years Education in Practice*. London: David Fulton.

Wilson, R. (2012) *Nature and Young Children: Encouraging Creative Play and Learning in Natural Environments*. London: David Fulton.

Woods, A. (ed.) (2016) *Examining Levels of Involvement in the Early Years: Engaging with Children's Possibilities*. London: David Fulton.

CHAPTER

9

Natural play connections

This closing chapter will explore well-established constructs of play and how elemental play may 'be judged by the extent to which [it] can be integrated or re-conceptualised with previous ones' (Vasta, 1992: 277). Kimes Myers (1997: 5–6) articulates the idea that *theories are edges*:

> Such exploration on the margins of what we know allows those who live and work with young children to accept the position of becoming informal researchers even as they explore this edge; that is, they might be investigating what we still don't know even as they ask questions related to the children in their care ... has the potential to move us beyond that inherited from those who came before.

The concept of elemental play has been 'bubbling on the edge' for many years, through observation of young children in many and diverse contexts: institutional, informal and familial, through reading, small-scale research, study and professional dialogue. Bird and Drewery (2003) reiterate this exploration, arguing

> We do not think that there is a universal body of knowledge about human development that is necessarily applicable to all people, so we are not intent upon either developing a universally generalisable theory, or offering 'the truth' about lifespan development.

What can be suggested, nevertheless, is that 'play is seen as a natural behavioural type' (van Oers, 2010: 196), and 'childhood as a time for play' (Brooker, 2010b: 39).

Natural elements for many cultures afford a rich environment for joint attention, sustained shared thinking and feeling and mutual cultural consciousness. Elemental play presents opportunities to explore:

- A sociocultural transitional perspective – as a two-way lifelong learning process from infancy through to adulthood and adults relating back to infancy.
- Mediated learning – adults mediating the continuity of natural experiences for children.
- Joint attention – and how this influences the interconnected relationship between infant and adult, in any culture and environment.
- Shared sustained thinking – and how this is outcome can also be an affective, mutual relationship between child and adult.
- Playfulness – a redefinition of free-play as natural playful learning where children encounter the world on their own terms.

This chapter focuses on play in early childhood. It is a daunting task. What is presented is a collection of 'all manner of things or elements that [have] "come in handy", selectively assorted and collected entities, [creating] an inventive assemblage or bricolage' (Taylor, 2013: 63). As bricoleur, the following ideas, suggestions and connections attempt to make sense of elemental play in relation to the preceding chapters, assimilated experiences as practitioners and academic and 'continually emerging possibilities' (Bird and Drewery, 2003), thus acknowledgement of every source and idea is virtually impossible to trace. What the elemental play model does offer, however, is *a rhizomatic model with which to deconstruct and reconstruct ideas by layering and use of multiple lenses*. It is a lateral rather than hierarchical model; it has a dynamic, flexible and lateral logic that encompasses change, complexity and context. Giugni (cited in MacNaughton, 2005: 110) proposes that our response to any ideas that cause a shift of ideas

> entails a splintering of the known and perhaps the 'truth'. Losinsky and Collinson (1999) argue that the response creates a phenomenological experience of the unexpected and chaotic; then the cognitive process of 'placing' the new knowledge within the displaced and fractured contextual understanding.

For us as adults, this process is similar to a child's *disequilibrium*; earlier assimilated understanding is accommodated in the light of new experience and knowledge. Using the lens of elemental play, it is intended, affords such a possibility and the following statements both frame this lens as well as foreground its key ideas.

Being playful

> *Playful investigation is instigated by a child within the context of people, places and things.*

Froebel presented us with an early view of play: 'Play becomes to the child the key to the world of things' (1912b, cited in Taylor, 2013: 41). Influenced by

Rousseau, reflecting Dewey and preceding Isaacs (1929, cited in Taylor, 2013: 133) who said 'Play has the greatest value for the child when it is really free and his own', both Froebel and Montessori 'promoted child-centred, experiential and play-based learning' (Taylor, 2013: 45). Smidt (2011: 2) reiterates: 'Play is thus always purposeful for the child'. She is not alone in identifying the agency, autonomy and control children demonstrate in their play. Hutt (1989), Garvey (1991), Goldschmeid and Jackson (1994), Bruce (2001) and Sylva et al. (2004) are identified as influential in Santer et al.'s (2007: 22) review, highlighting these common threads throughout the literature:

- Play is pleasurable and enjoyable.
- Play is intrinsically motivated and without extrinsic goals.
- Play is spontaneous and freely chosen.
- Play entails active engagement by the player.
- Play is systematically related to creativity, problem-solving, language-learning and the development of social roles.

Wood (2010), Brooker (2010a), Moyles (2010), Bodrova and Leong (2011) and Taylor (2013) continue to *trouble* the notion of play, particularly with regards to play and pedagogy, the dichotomy of learning through play and teaching through play, a contemporary concern of many early years practitioners and academics.

This concern helps to qualify the initial statement. Brooker (2010a: 29) cites Göncü et al., 2006: 175):

> Play is a universal characteristic, not only of children but of all humans, but the ways that children play vary according to economic, social and cultural contexts. Theories of play should be situated in children's contexts, taking into account [the] unique dimensions of children's specific communities.

Elemental play acknowledges that where, when, with what and for how long a young child plays is usually out of their own control, but can still be described as play. The mode of investigation *may* be within a child's agency, but is *highly dependent upon the power that adults are ready, willing and able to share.* A cultural context is universal but the universality varies throughout the individual ecological systems that Bronfenbrenner identified as shaping the child's development and learning. The context is crucial to early child development and sits within a socio-constructivist model. May et al. (2006: 105) concur:

> if every child's experience is seen as unique, we need to think beyond the biological development of the child. We need to think about the child's developmental interaction with the child's specific social and cultural context. Research shows that context affects cognition, socio-emotional and emotional well-being, educational achievement and life chances.

Vygotsky (1978: 103) also reminds us that it is not just the context of play activity, but also the cultural significance of the object at the centre of play activity: 'In one sense a child at play is free to determine his own actions. But in another sense this is an illusory freedom, for his actions are in fact subordinated to the meanings of things, and he acts accordingly.'

Children's play

> *How children play is unique to them, but reflects context and 'memory in action'. Play is returned to and repeated but unique in the present play objective of the child/children. This objective is closely related to the people, places and things they have and are experiencing. Open-ended play with loose materials and objects that can be multi-functional, affords children creative possibilities.*

We have recognised that play is purposeful for the child. Vygotsky (1978) again reminds us that

> Play is more nearly recollection of something that has actually happened than imagination. It is more memory in action than a novel imaginary situation. As play develops, we see a movement toward the conscious realization of its purpose. Purpose, as the ultimate goal, determines the child's affective attitude to play.

Bruce (2001) concurs: 'children try out their most recent learning, skills and competencies. They seem to celebrate what they know.' Eaude (2006: 71) also reminds us of Winnicott (1980) who 'places great emphasis on the child making meaning through activity. The learner needs to play, to be playful, to try things out and to experience what a newly constructed or imagined reality looks and feels like from within, without bearing the consequences.'

The form of children's play is discussed and described as frequently as the function of children's play. What we have explored in earlier chapters is the evidence of children's repeated, perhaps schematic, playful behaviour with natural materials specifically; play that is sensual, tactile, exploratory, scientific and reminiscent of playful activity in previous generations. The play usually involves loose parts which lend themselves to make meaning from the open-ended play that emerges, and often mimicking a memory of activity with other cultural artefacts – a stick for a sword, a wooden brick for a phone, or a wooden disc for a snail's bed.

In the following Encounter, the brothers Steve and Simon show that they are familiar with plane travel to holiday destinations; they also seem to have some knowledge of rudimentary and mechanical features of driving/flying a plane. This is Vygotsky's memory in action, but their unique use of the branches in the wood and their present play scenario demonstrates Winnicott's making meaning. The branches and space in the woodland afforded them the possibility to connect their ideas and memories and transform past experiences into new play actions. Playing, here, is re-creation. The twin brothers were very comfortable in the woodland;

> **ENCOUNTER: Steve and Simon using what they know in their play**
>
> There are a great number of boughs to use in the woods – of different lengths, all transportable by one, or usually two children. I notice that the brothers have begun to lay some boughs out in a grid-like pattern in the clearing. They appear to be working to a definite idea although there is little shared discussion apart from 'let's find two longer and a number of shorter pieces to make a ladder'. The grid becomes their aeroplane. They sit on the seat – a thicker piece of bough and rest a shorter bough across their laps ... and take off. The short bough is a gear/steering prop. The accompanying noises are of a motor. The noise stops, the prop is lifted and put to one side – rather like a constraining bar on a fairground ride. The brothers climb over (down) the ladder talking to themselves about climbing down from the plane and go on holiday. They return to the plane, take off and repeat the flight play a number of times before finally reaching 'their destination'.
>
> *Source*: Woods (2015: 58)

they returned each week, always first to a particular tree, and subsequently engaged in close imaginary and physical play. Their home was a small farm and they continued to enjoy the environmental freedoms of forest school where they could play within their own time frames and resources on offer. It was deeply involved play with high levels of well-being, play that would have been challenging to offer inside.

Rich (2003, cited in Santer et al., 2007: 31) summarises play as reflecting:

- What they have experienced.
- What they are interested in.
- What they know about (to the limits of their knowledge).
- What they want to know more about.
- What they want to understand;.
- What they are anxious, concerned or worried over.
- What they feel.
- Their many possible future roles.

Kaarby (n.d.: 126) goes further when concluding her research on observing children in outdoor play:

> Quality can be understood as the meaning or value a phenomenon has to those who are involved (Dahlberg et al., 1999; Søbstad, 2004). I have tried to describe how the wild environment influences children's play and, from my

point of view, gives value to play. I have tried to describe how nature was a dominant element in all kinds of play, and how children perceive functions of the environment and use them (Heft, 1988). Because of the seasons, the landscape has different characteristics and affords different functions during the year. These different features give various options and great diversity. The creativity children showed when transforming objects was conspicuous. While some will say that the environment simply serves the play, another way of looking at it is to ask how the environment created the play, how a feature invited just that particular kind of play.

Social construction of childhood

> *We can infer what children are doing, thinking or trying, but our interpretation is grounded in our values, beliefs and developing social construction of childhood.*

Earlier in the chapter, the sharing of power between adults and children was introduced as part of the socio-constructivism of elemental play. Foucault's work explores the relationships between knowledge, truth and power and the effects of these relationships on us. MacNaughton (2005: 30–1) cites Gore (1998), who drew on Foucault to identify eight 'micropractices of power' that can be mapped against key ideas in the concept of elemental play:

- *Surveillance* – we use the lens of observation to interpret behaviour, including play behaviours. How we observe, and the parameters of any observation *schemes* reflect a truth or construction of childhood that as practitioners we have absorbed.
- *Normalisation* – observation normally conforms to developmental/comparative or measurable outcomes; the tool normalises what we see, for example, schema or levels of involvement. The elemental model permits the child to be seen in relation to a self-determined focus with regards to people, places and things.
- *Exclusion* – the elemental play model reduces the pathology of observed abnormal/undesirable behaviour and activity, empowering the child and child/adult dynamic, and thus is inclusive in its aims.
- *Classification* – elemental play only differentiates in the child's interests and relationships, not goals, outcomes or abilities. It empowers us to extend rather than inhibit children's emerging relationships and ideas.
- *Distribution* – elemental play does not order children into developmental stages.
- *Individualisation* – assessment and observation can and does allow us to separate children according to individual needs and establish a *compensatory* programme; what the lens of elemental play allows us to do is establish an environment where children's preferences can be met. These preferences can be recognised by attuned adults, those who can empower children and encourage exploratory 'forays' with people, places and things.

- *Totalisation* – observation and consequent action engenders conformity. Elemental play theory respects and extends non-conformity (Brown, in Woods, 2013; Moran, in Woods, 2015; Gripton, in Woods, 2016).
- *Regulation* – if the lens through which we observe and measure children confines their behaviour and self-determined journeys and routines, to what extent may we inhibit children's own knowledge and constructions about people, places and things, their moral and spiritual responsibilities and potential for finding their own solutions?

Observations of children and how they appear to begin their journeys into playfulness through relating to people, or a space/place in an environment or with certain objects or ideas led to the emergence of the *elemental play model as a way of explaining what they might be doing*. Through continued dialogue and discussion, and connections found in many established theories and ideas, the scope of its potential grew; it is a different lens through which to look at what children are doing, but not an assessment tool to measure or classify their behaviour. The connections made and a construction of childhood presented is a particular direction taken that results from reflecting on experiences and early years practitioner enculturation. Brooker (2010b: 43) confirms this: 'the material arrangements of children's activities and responsibilities are the physical embodiment of our beliefs about learning, and are very often grounded in the importance of play for childhood'. Vasta (1992: 280), when discussing learning theories, is also reassuring in relation to re-envisaging play when so much has previously been written:

> Many aspects of child development can be more fully understood if an appreciation of the child's initial propensities, including its learning predispositions, is brought together with a functional approach, with its capability for integrating diverse facts about human development into a cohesive framework. It is necessary also for the analysis to cross and re-cross the successive levels of social complexity, and to take cognizance both of the influence of cultural forces on the developing child and the genesis of those cultural forces themselves.

Kimes Myers (1997: 8–10) is also supportive of acknowledging how our own experiences shape our view of childhood and play, both social constructs open to interpretation:

> Erikson (1964) suggests that we and our children meet at our own particular age or stage of development even as we interactively move each other along. He terms this interactive process 'cogwheeling'. His work encourages us to recognize that when we engage with young children the child within us also has a developing edge that enters into our newly emerging relationship with these young people. This awareness gifts us with the ability to empathize with children, to play with them, and to consider options for guiding and teaching them. It also challenges us to think about what we are like and what we want

our children to be like. Through such 'cogwheeling', they participate in a relational developmental dialogue of their own creation, not in any lock step way, but fluently from the depth of lived experience within the social context and historical space of their time.

Play is active

> *Play is both an action and activity – play can be defined, seen as a model of learning, and observed in the exploration and experimentation of children. In playing, children are actively engaging with people, places and things.*

'Moyles (2005) regards play as a multi-faceted layer of activities' (Santer et al., 2007: 7). Moyles (2010: 28) later expands on this, offering a distillation of many recent ideas and thoughts about play:

> Play in all its forms is a powerful scaffold for children's learning: it enables metacognition (learning about how to understand one's own learning and play). It allows children to cope with not knowing something long enough in order to know – they can rehearse, practise, revise, replay and re-learn . . . It frees them from worrying about doing things wrong and gives them confidence to try out alternatives. Children learn to establish their own identity and their place in order to interrogate the world in which they find themselves without loss of self-esteem and, above all, play enables children to learn that learning is – and should always be – enjoyable, personally profitable and challenging; this is the vital feature if we are to have happy and well-balanced flexible learners and citizens of the future.

Elemental play acknowledges play as a process and mode of learning, a way of doing something; it is seen particularly as a way of finding out about the world and the child's place within the world of people, places and things. This seems to be fundamental to the development of children within their culture and their continued, successful part they both play and will play *in the dynamic ecological systems of the world around them*. As Winnicott (1971: 55) suggests: 'To control what is outside [the self] one has to *do* things, not simply to think or to wish, and *doing things takes time*. Playing is doing.' Playing is not passive; engaging with ideas involves cognitive and imaginative activity:

> We come to know through processes of active interpretation and integration. We ask questions, which may or may not be out into words and which may or may not be addressed to other people. We have strategies of many kinds for finding out. We struggle – and it can be a long, hard struggle – to make sense. The notion that we make our own systems of knowledge has been strongly advocated by Jean Piaget. According to him the development of the mind consists largely in the building of 'cognitive structures' and the rebuilding

of these structures in new and better integrated forms over long periods of time (1969).

(Donaldson, 1992: 19)

Elemental play reflects both constructivist and socio-constructivist approaches as we have observed children building their own knowledge of the world through *active and reciprocal exploration through the relationships and guidance* of more mature others. Indeed, it is these relationships that form the centre of the elemental play model (see Figure 1.1, Chapter 1).

What has been linked, in Chapter 4, is that children's playful activity includes a metaphysical and spiritual dimension through regular exploration of the natural world, engaging with ideas and objects and through the cultural heritage of their communities: 'It *re-envisages the actions of very young children from an innate, spiritual and ecological developmental perspective*' (Ryder, pers. comm., 2016). 'As Hakkarainen (2006) points out, play is an intrinsically motivated process with outcomes and developmental effects that are not always immediately visible' (Broadhead et al., 2010: 178).

Play and creativity

To be playful is to be creative; being creative is to be curious and being curious is risky.

It was Locke who first wrote about children's predisposition to be curious (Santer et al., 2007: 2). The authors also summarise from the literature that 'risk-taking can be regarded as an intelligent behaviour, because creative people have been observed to place themselves in situations where they do not know what is going to happen' (p. 44). Tovey (2010: 80) succinctly sums up her attitude to risk in saying 'risk should be considered a characteristic of play itself as children seek to push boundaries, try things out, toy with ideas and explore the unknown'. Winnicott (1971: 73) suggests 'it is in playing and only in playing that the individual child or adult is able to be creative and to use the whole personality, and it is only in being creative that the individual discovers the self'. This is adventurous and scary, and can be mysterious, exciting and open-ended, like taking a journey and not quite knowing where it will end; the journey process being the playful element. Tovey reflects Tizard and Hughes (1984, cited by May et al., 2006: 50) who suggest that 'humans are born explorers; they are curious and have inbuilt need to know. This natural curiosity can be nurtured or in unfavourable circumstances it can be stifled.' This is not just physical playful curiosity. They add:

> If a child is to grow into a self-assured adult, then one of the important aspects of their progress is the development of confidence in movement. This is part and parcel of growing up, as the child not only learns about their own physical

capability but also learns about their own existence in space, their place in the physical world and the relationships between themselves and others.

(Ibid.: 51)

Becoming de-linked from the environment is a contemporary concern of Louv (2005, 2102) who writes about nature-deficit disorder and delinquent risk-taking, which although part of curious behaviour can also be destructive, unsociable and dangerous. White and Woolley (2014: 29) cite Holt (1990) who also warns that 'Children are born passionately eager to make as much sense as they can of things around them . . . if we attempt to control, manipulate, or divert this process . . . the independent scientist in the child disappears.'

Riley (2012) reminds us:

> Duffy's (2006) description of a creative process has four elements: curiosity (becoming interested in what it is); exploration (investigating what it can do); play (immersion to find out what I can do with this); and, creativity (what can I create or invent with this).

Here, play with objects is foregrounded but Kaarby (n.d.: 122, 126) goes further:

> Children perceive the functions of the features in the environment, and they intuitively use them for physical challenges and play, [. . .] corresponding to the individual's strength, skills, courage and fear. While some will say that the environment simply serves the play, another way of looking is to ask how the environment created the play, how a feature invited just that particular kind of play.

Elemental play celebrates individual children's relationship with people, places and things. Ryder, in earlier chapters, discussed how some children felt unease, or at risk, in a new environment and would seek a familiar person, or a place or an object to help the transition between home and early years setting. Risk, here, is not seen as dangerous, but unknown, and a situation to be managed by children themselves, similar to problem-solving, or by adults attuned to children's unease and hesitancy. It is different from avoiding a hazard, which may be injurious to health:

> we have problemetized discourse around risk in relation to differing but contemporaneous conceptualizations of childhood, arguing that adopting a fixed view of the universal child fails to acknowledge the messiness and complexity of situated, cultural and individual responses to risk and security.

(Waite et al., 2014: 81)

For children to be well and to find their way in current times, they need opportunities to take risks, to run, to leap, shout and be messy, in a way rarely possible indoors. In an increasingly 'virtual' world they also need to explore with their senses the physical elements of the environment. They need opportunities to observe and experience first-hand some of the amazing features of the planet on which they depend for survival. Space and time for outdoor learning in the early years can help children discover who they are and make sense of the world.

(Davy, n.d.)

We may argue, therefore, that risk-taking is a positive, evolutionary behaviour securing the physical, emotional and high-functioning elements of societies and their continued development and success in relation to the elements such as fire, earth, air and water, and the holistic entanglement of human and non-human species.

Observing play

Through observation, we can see repeated behaviours, emerging ideas, schematic play and high levels of involvement when children are afforded time to 'wallow' in playful activity.

In the previous chapters, and through a number of encounters with children, elemental play has been explored. This exploration follows a discourse first introduced in *Child-Initiated Play and Learning* (Woods, 2013) and continued in *Characteristics of Effective Learning* (2015), where authors propose that the pedagogical ethos is one of playfulness, for all children and adults. We may define playful as actively engaging with unique ways of feeling, thinking and doing whether this is transporting water in a teapot to the sand tray or creating and sharing a new administrative routine. Consistent themes have emerged in three edited books (Woods, 2013, 2015, 2016), reflecting a socio-constructive perspective, the idea that learning takes place mainly through the interaction with others; in these current chapters, a re-conceptualising of attachment theory has been considered as attachment can be to environment as well as adult or transitional object. The child is seen as leader, learning independently, with peers and/or alongside adults attuned to reciprocal and valued relationships. The possibilities envisaged of active play and learning represent the child as fully participatory, a child with voice, autonomy and competence, learning with environments that afford an infinite number of possibilities. In this book, the *named* concept of elemental play has been explored further to consider *the repeated patterns of relational behaviour seen in very young children, and the time they enjoy in experiential discoveries; elemental play advocates for the natural experiences of the very young child.* The experiences with natural resources and in wilder environments are significant both in the encounters in the preceding chapters and through research described in *Examining Levels of Involvement in the Early Years* (Woods, 2016).

Sharing the time frame of children is also key to children becoming powerful learners. *Elemental play champions the mutuality of reciprocal and playful exploration.*

Imaginary play

> *Vygotsky claimed that in imaginary play, children show their zone of proximal development and by symbolic activity are expressing complex ideas. Playing or working through inexperience of an object or idea is both a human and a high-functioning species trait.*

In Chapters 6 and 7, children's imaginary play outside and the ideas they begin to *play around* with were explored and illustrated both with observations and examples from researchers. Hay and Nye (2006: 73) recognise 'the free use of imagination [as] very evident in children's play'. The value of loose parts, easily found in wilder, outdoor environments afford many and diverse opportunities for children to play in ways that often surprise us as they transform objects symbolically to represent their playful ideas. Naming areas such as the 'swamp monster', 'lying tree', 'trampoline tree' and 'goblin cave' demonstrate that children are building a sense of themselves within an environment and beginning to relate to the cultural milieu in which they are apprenticed to through symbolic interconnectedness and continued reification of objects, characters and stories they have experienced. Van Oers (2010: 197) suggests that Leont'ev (1981a), a post-Vygotskian academic, 'articulates that play does not originate from fantasy, but emerges as a way to accomplish activities wherein the child participates'. Using symbols indicates a degree of developing abstract thought, and it is this disposition towards creativity and emergent problem-solving that continues to distinguish humans as a high-functioning species. One of the phenomenological ideas behind *elemental play is the notion of 'elevating the mental' (ele-mental), lifting mental, cultural and environmental awareness*. Bodrova and Leong (2011: 61) cite Vygotsky (1967) as suggesting

> Play is the source of development and creates the zone of proximal development. Action in the imaginary sphere, in an imaginary situation, the creation of voluntary intentions and the formation of real-life plans and volitional motives – all appear in play and make it the highest level of present development.

Moyles (2010: 245) adds: 'Vygotsky (1967) suggested that during play children experiment with the cultural meanings and rules of life, freeing themselves from everyday constraints.' Exploration is essential to understand the world; Hutt (1989, cited in Manning-Morton and Thorpe, 2003) described this as epistemic play and later Goldschmeid and Jackson (1994) illuminated heuristic play characteristics in children as evident in purposeful experimenting with loose materials. This experimentation and exploration is often talked about as a natural behaviour in childhood. Jarvis (2010: 64) cites Mallon and Stich (2000) as they describe this as bioculturalism:

> [the] biocultural model . . . reflects a confluence between innate and learned influences. The more complex and flexible the adult society, the longer

animals spend in their juvenile, pre-adult period, and the more complex and flexible the play activities in which they engage.

Taylor (2013: 118) alludes to bioculturalism when she talks of

> a common worlds approach [which] include nonhuman living and nonhuman inert entities and elements that are typically separated into the 'nature' camp – other animals, plants, weather, water and 'natural' materials – already entangled cohabitants.

She is persuasive when problemetising the

> Child-centred focus on a child's individuality and their developing autonomous agency [running] counter to the task of appreciating that no-one stands or acts alone, that all human lives are inextricably enmeshed with others and that all human actions are implicated with and have implications for others (human and more-than-human).
>
> (Ibid.: 117)

In Chapter 1, the *concept of elemental play constructed as an instinctive, human and cultural disposition* recognises the motivation that is present when children choose the relationship they can establish with people, places and things, and enables us to more fully encompass the enduring socio-constructivist ideology of Vygotsky as well as acknowledge the world children inhabit. Gray (2013: 174) considers that 'we seriously under-estimate children's ability to take care of themselves and make good judgements. In this respect, we differ not just from hunter-gatherer cultures but from all traditional cultures in which children played freely.' *Elemental play celebrates children's abilities to establish such judgements in their cultural environment.*

Play is instinctive

> *Play appears to be what a species do instinctively to survive and evolve, and for humans, this supports the development of knowledge and understanding of the cultural context.*

Hughes (2001) writes persuasively about an evolutionary play instinct, a shared biological heritage, present among mammals and evolving in its complexity through natural selection and adaptation where sophisticated mental structures further develop new combinations of thought and action in exploratory activity. *Elemental play connects to eco-psychology and evolutionary play-work* very closely and it is always fascinating to encounter parallel ideas when thinking through and interpreting observations of children's play behaviours. Santer et al. (2007: 23, 40) acknowledge Hughes (2001) as defining 'Play as the actions of a lone child carrying out evolutionary behaviour by seeking to establish links with other humans, species and systems, following the pattern set out in evolution', citing Bailey (1999: 47) in agreement, 'play evolved as a process by which the body was prepared for the challenges likely to befall it'.

Many ideas expressed about play describe its future function. Bjorkland and Pellegrini (2002: 321) cite Kagan (1996) who 'suggested that Piaget and Vygotsky proposed that the benefits of play are understood in terms of what good it does in later development. Bateson (1976) has referred to this as the "*scaffolding* view of play".' Bodrova and Leong (2011: 63) cite Elkonin (2005b) where he concludes

> In the non-literate societies of hunter-gatherer, play existed as preparation for grown up activities as children practiced with scaled-down versions of grown-up tools. Play helps today's children develop general competencies that will allow them to master the use of any tools of the future – even ones not yet invented.

Elemental play integrates with Hughes' evolutionary play theory, Wilson's biophilia and the 'commonworlds' approach of Taylor. Brooker cites Slaughter and Dombrowski (1989) (2010a: 29) who also state '[play] appears sustained as an evolutionary contribution to human psychological growth and development'. Gray (2013: 119) offers further connections 'from a biological/evolutionary perspective, play is nature's way of ensuring that young mammals including young humans, with practice can become good at the skills they need to develop to survive and thrive on their own'. Kellert (1993: 21) articulates that biophilia is:

- a human inclination to affiliate with life and life-like processes is inherent (biologically based);
- part of our species' evolutionary heritage;
- associated with human competitive advantage and genetic fitness;
- likely to increase the possibility for achieving individual meaning and personal fulfilment;
- a self-interested basis for a human ethic of care and conservation of nature, most especially the diversity of life.

Heerwagen and Orians (1993: 139) concur:

> If we regard the human brain as an evolved organ especially designed to analyse and respond appropriately to the opportunities and constraints that existed in ancestral environments, we begin to look at human interactions with the natural world in a new way. Our ancestors' . . . survival, health, and reproductive success depended on their ability to seek and use environmental information wisely. They had to know how to interpret signals from the animate and inanimate environments and how to adjust their behavioural response to the context at hand.

The elemental play model helps us to accomplish this. Earlier chapters have remarked on the similar, natural play behaviours of children as they begin to explore the natural world, building, creating shelters, digging holes, bridging streams, testing their physical skills and transforming objects through symbolic play. The majority of these activities have been present over many generations and appear to be culturally instinctive. It reflects Greenman (1988: 286) who states 'Human beings evolved outdoors. Our bodies need sunlight and fresh air. Our minds need the experiences and challenges that nature presents. Our souls need the day to day appreciation for the miracle of the world and all its complexity.' Faarlund (2007: 60) concludes:

> Children who do not get the chance to play in the rich diversity of free nature become strangers in life. Play is important for life. Play in nature is the road to the understanding that the nature is the home of the culture. The human value, as well as the nature value, is lost without the play in the free nature.

Communities of learners

> *In communities of learners, children are encouraged to find out what an object does, and what can be done with an object. Guided participation within a dynamic ecology of cultural systems is the means by which this happens. Elemental play involves the evolving and investigative relationship between people, places and things that reflect both the elements and elemental forces enveloping the child.*

Evolutionary play theory suggests that when early human society learned to use materials and tools to more easily survive, the objects became in turn cultural artefacts valued and modified by future generations. Marfo and Biersteker (2011: 74) suggest that:

> Play is a mechanism for enculturation (Schwartzman, 1978) – children model substantial aspects of their play on adult activities (Kamp, 2001) and in so doing, learn not only the social roles and cultural values and norms typical in the culture but also the skills and competencies necessary for survival and productive community membership.

Learning to use materials and tools is agreed to be a main facet of children's exploratory play, and Rogoff (1990: 18) described 'learning as the transformation of participation in cultural activities'. She further argues and evidences through research:

> Guided participation involves adults or children challenging, constraining and supporting children in the process of posing and solving problems – through material arrangements of children's activities and responsibilities as well as though interpersonal communication, with children observing and participating at a comfortable but slightly challenging level.
>
> Cognitive development, in other words, occurs in the course of 'children's everyday involvement of social life', including their intent participation in all

the activities which they see other children, and adults, performing. Such participation depends for its effectiveness on the *intersubjectivity* [her italics] or 'shared understanding' which exists between the expert and the novice.

Children enter the world embedded in an interpersonal system involving their caregivers and others who are already involved with societal institutions and technologies. Through guided participation with others, children come to understand and participate in the skilled activities of their culture.

(Ibid.: 18, 71, 191)

Elkonin (1978, cited by van Oers, 2010: 200) concurs: 'Play is the cultural invention that makes adult practices accessible for young children.' This accessibility happens within communities of learners, the micro and meso-layers of Bronfenbrenner's ecological systems theory; family and community are the people children relate to in the elemental play model. It is a socio-cultural and transitional perspective on learning and development which interconnects infancy to adulthood and adults to children. In Chapter 2, the idea that *elemental play may explain the exploratory activity of young children as they discover, seek, accept and reject both natural and found materials* was explored. It was argued that this occurred through nurturing and reciprocal relationships with adults whose role is it to welcome them into the cultural world around them. The cultural world also includes what Moore and Young (1978: 84, 90) name as the

> three interdependent realms of experience: the physiological-psychological environment of body/mind; the sociological environment of interpersonal relations and cultural values; and the physiographic landscape of spaces, objects, persons, and natural and built elements. Children's phenomenal landscapes [include]:
>
> - *Territorial range* – the collective spatial realm of experiential breadth and diversity.
> - *Place* – the locus of experiential depth and involvement and the source of knowledge and affiliation.
> - *Pathway* – the conjoining network component, threading place and territory together, emphasizing mobility and experiential continuity.

Knowledge and understanding of community landscape was explored in Chapter 3 and presented as clearly linked to a child's growing identity of who they are and where they belong. *Elemental play is a process of finding out about oneself in relation to the people, places and things in their own landscape.* In Chapter 1, it was argued, a child is drawn to and demonstrates well-being when playing in a natural context that is culturally and ecologically familiar:

> A conclusion that stands out is the evident cultural dependency of children's outdoor relationships. The impression is strong enough to suggest that every subculture has a significant ethos in childhood environmental experience

(Young, 1975). Interrelated with cultural dependencies there also exist, theoretically, more universal species-specific developmental functions, facilitated or constrained as a result of children's outdoor experience; '...under appropriate ecological conditions children themselves will reveal environmental dependencies that lie beyond the conditioning effects of the particular culture they were born into'.

(Ibid.: 122–3)

The particular culture is an effective community of learners: 'involving active learners and more skilled partners who provide leadership and guidance – learning involves transformation of participation in collaborative endeavour' (Rogoff et al., 1996: 388).

Such a transformation sees a child's performance in culturally valued activities [cooking, gardening, singing rhymes and retelling stories, reading, playing an instrument, for example] change over time from that of novice to that of expert, as a result of drawing on the affordances of the environment, under the guidance of more experienced individuals.

(Brooker, 2010b: 41)

Haakarainen's (Engstrom et al., 1999: 247) idea that 'What seems to be totally independent play of children at the moment was initiated, guided and instructed by perhaps years ago. The adults' own play experiences influence which play themes are selected and how they are set up and guided.' It is interesting to observe interactions between adults and children and where important interactions take place, with Needham (2011: 56) adding: 'Studies of children's learning from early infancy onwards draw attention to the nature of the interactions between adults and children as a key indicator of effective learning.'

This book has been an exploration of a number of ideas connected to instinctive natural play, going beyond what children like to play with, how they play and the provision we make for young children in our settings. Encounters have illustrated children's instincts, extraordinary imagination, inquiries and developing connections with the wilder environment and these, alongside reflective conversations with colleagues, should encourage us to think positively about the idea of elemental play.

The theory of elemental play asserts that the developing child makes sense of self in relation to the natural environment through the social and cultural reciprocity of familiar people, places and things. It is an interpretative, dynamic, ecological model of a child's early development grounded in the nurture, protection and shared cultural values of communities embedded in an evolutionary past, present and future. Elemental play theory recognises a spiritual component to child development through the role of the natural environment in the particular community of people in a specific landscape who construct stories, sense mystery, develop understanding and make meaning together. By formalising elemental play, we can re-conceptualise how important regular access to and experience of *being outdoors* is to children and value the role as environmental advocates we should adopt, for those young enough to show us, but perhaps not tell us, how crucial experiential play with natural materials is to their being, becoming and belonging to an evolving human race.

Provocations

- What stimulates the adult to want to mediate the child's learning process with natural elements?
- Why might some adults affiliate more easily than others with this concept of mediating learning in relation to the natural world?
- Valleys, streams, hills and trees are a constant, with small, evolutionary changes such as the streams finding new ways to overflow the land; to what extent do you think whether there is a primeval/elemental connection to that which was always there?
- Play activity seen by most of us in very young children seems to be very similar, built upon in each generation, but not copied as adults do not play like children; where does this natural/elemental play come from?
- Can elemental play be part of a collective and cultural, spiritual memory?
- Try and define play in your own words.
- If children are to become active researchers, they need the opportunity to play. Play is children's active construction of knowledge and understanding where the child is permitted to choose what to do. Where and with what, does most of the play happen in your setting?
- The ability to play does not seem to disappear; elemental play suggests it is not a linear but an environmental barrier that appears to gradually erode the possibilities to engage in exploration. Discuss any perceived barriers in your own practice or environment.

References

Bird, L. and Drewery, W. (2003) Between a flax and a mangrove: theories of human development for Aotearoa. Paper presented to the AARE/NZARE Conference, Auckland, December.

Bjorkland, D.F. and Pellegrini, A.D. (2002) *The Origins of Human Nature: Evolutionary Developmental Psychology*. Washington, DC: American Psychological Association.

Bodrova, E. and Leong, D.J. (2011). Revisiting Vygotskian perspectives on play and pedagogy. In S. Rogers (ed.) *Rethinking Play and Pedagogy in Early Childhood Education: Concepts, Contexts and Cultures*. London: Routledge.

Broadhead, P., Howard, J. and Wood, E. (2010) Conclusion: understanding playful learning and playful pedagogies – towards a new research agenda. In P. Broadhead, J. Howard and E. Wood (eds) *Play and Learning in the Early Years*. London: Sage, pp. 177–86.

Brooker, L. (2010a) Learning to play in a cultural context. In P. Broadhead, J. Howard and E. Wood (eds) *Play and Learning in the Early Years*. London: Sage, pp. 27–42.

Brooker, L. (2010b) Learning to play, or playing to learn? Children's participation in the cultures of homes and settings. In L. Brooker and S. Edwards, *Engaging Play*. Maidenhead: Open University Press, pp. 39–53.

Bruce, T. (2001) *Learning through Play: Babies, Toddlers and the Foundation Years*. London: Hodder and Stoughton.

Davy, A. (n.d.) Changing landscapes changing children's lives. www.ltl.org.uk/resources/results.php?id=825 (accessed 12 August 2015).

Donaldson, M. (1992) *Human Minds. An Exploration*. London: Penguin.

Eaude, T. (2006) *Children's Spiritual, Moral, Social and Cultural Development. Primary and Early Years*. Exeter: Learningmatters.

Engström, Y., Miettinen, R. and Punamaki, R.-L. (eds) (1999) *Perspectives in Activity Theory*. New York: Cambridge University Press.

Faarlund, N. (2007) Defining friluftsliv. In B. Henderson and N. Vikander (eds) *Nature First. Outdoor Life the Friluftsliv Way*. Toronto: Natural Heritage Books, pp. 56–61.

Goldschmeid, E. and Jackson, S. (1994) *People Under Three. Young Children in Day Care*. London: Routledge.

Gray, P. (2013) *Free to Learn. Why Unleashing the Instinct to Play Will Make Our Children Happier, More Self-reliant and Better Students for Life*. New York: Basic Books.

Greenman, J. (1988) *Caring Spaces, Learning Places: Children's Environments That Work*. Redmond, WA: Exchange Press.

Hay, D. with Nye, R. (2006) *The Spirit of the Child*, rev. edn. London: Jessica Kingsley.

Heerwagen, J.H. and Orians, G.H. (1993) Humans, habitats and aesthetics. In S.R. Kellert and E.O. Wilson (eds) *The Biophilia Hypothesis*. Washington, DC: Shearwater Books, pp. 138–72.

Hughes, B. (2001) *Evolutionary Playwork*, 2nd edn. London: Routledge.

Jarvis, P. (2010) 'Born to play': the biocultural roots of rough and tumble play, and its impact upon young children's learning and development. In P. Broadhead, J. Howard and E. Wood (eds) *Play and Learning in the Early Years*. London: Sage, pp. 61–78.

Kaarby, K.M.E. (n.d.) Children playing in nature. www.cecde.ie/english/pdf/Questions%20of%20Quality/Kaarby.pdf (accessed 14 September 2015).

Kellert, S. R. (1993) Introduction. In S.R. Kellert and E.O. Wilson (eds) *The Biophilia Hypothesis*. Washington, DC: Island Press/Shearwater Books.

Kellert, S.R. and Wilson, E.O. (eds) (1993) *The Biophilia Hypothesis*. Washington, DC: Shearwater Books.

Kimes Myers, B. (1997) *Young Children and Spirituality*. London: Routledge.

Louv, R. (2005) *Last Child in the Woods. Saving Our Children from Nature-Deficit Disorder*. Chapel Hill, NC: Alonquin.

Louv, R. (2012) *The Nature Principle. Reconnecting with Life in a Virtual Age*. Chapel Hill, NC: Alonquin.

MacNaughton, G. (2005) *Doing Foucault in Early Childhood Studies: Applying Poststructural Ideas*. London: Routledge.

Manning-Morton, J. and Thorpe, M. (2003) *Key Times for Play: The First Three Years*. Maidenhead: Open University Press.

Marfo, K. and Biersteker, L. (2011) Exploring culture, play, and early childhood education practice in African contexts. In S. Rogers (ed.) *Rethinking Play and Pedagogy in Early Childhood Education: Concepts, Contexts and Cultures*. London: Routledge, pp. 73–85.

May, P., Ashford, E. and Bottle, G. (2006) *Sound Beginnings: Learning and Development in the Early Years*. London: David Fulton.

Moore, R. and Young, D. (1978) Childhood outdoors: towards a social ecology of the landscape. In I. Altman and J.F. Wohlwill (eds) *Human Behaviour and Environment, Advances in Theory and Research. Vol. 3: Children and the Environment*. New York: Plenum Press, pp. 83–130.

Moyles, J. (2010) *The Excellence of Play*, 3rd edn. Maidenhead: Open University Press.

Needham, M. (2011) Using activity theory to examine the factors shaping the learning partnership in a parent and child 'stay and play' session. In T. Waller, J. Whitmarsh and K. Clarke (eds) *Making Sense of Theory and Practice in Early Childhood*. Maidenhead: McGraw Hill/Open University Press, pp. 54–68.

Riley, M. (2012) Forest school: how creative processes impact on emotional wellbeing. *Horizons* (59) Autumn. www.outdoor-learning.org/Portals/0/IOL%20Documents/Horizons%20Documents/Horizons%20pdf%20archive/H59.ForestSchool.CreativeProcesses.Emotional Wellbeing.pdf (accessed 14 September 2015).

Rogoff, B. (1990) *Apprenticeship in Thinking. Cognitive Development in Social Context*. Oxford: Oxford University Press.

Rogoff, B., Matusov, E. and White, C. (1996) *Handbook of Education and Human Development*. Oxford: Blackwell.

Santer, J., Griffiths, C. and Goodall, D. (2007) *Free Play in Early Childhood. A Literature Review*. London: National Children's Bureau.

Smidt, S. (2011) *Playing to Learn: The Role of Play in the Early Years*. London: Routledge.

Taylor, A. (2013) *Reconfiguring the Natures of Childhood*. London: Routledge.

Tovey, H. (2010) Playing on the edge: perceptions of risk and danger in outdoor play. In P. Broadhead, J. Howard and E. Wood (eds) *Play and Learning in the Early Years*. London: Sage, pp. 77–94.

van Oers, B. (2010) Children's enculturation through play. In L. Brooker and S. Edwards (eds) *Engaging Play*. Maidenhead: Open University Press, pp. 195–209.

Vasta, R. (ed.) (1992) *Six Theories of Child Development: Revised Formulations and Current Issues*. London: Jessica Kingsley.

Vygotsky, L. (1978) *Mind in Society: The Development of Higher Psychological Processes*. Cambridge, MA: Harvard University Press.

Waite, S., Huggins, H. and Wickett, K. (2014) Risky outdoor play: embracing uncertainty in pursuit of learning. In T. Maynard and J. Waters (eds) *Exploring Outdoor Play in the Early Years*. Maidenhead: Open University Press, pp. 71–85.

White, J. and Woolley, H. (2014) What makes a good outdoor environment for young children? In T. Maynard and J. Waters (eds) *Exploring Outdoor Play in the Early Years*. Maidenhead: Open University Press, pp. 29–41.

Winnicott, D. (1971) *Playing and Reality*. London and New York: Routledge.

Wood, E. (2010) Developing integrated pedagogical approaches to play and learning. In P. Broadhead, J. Howard and E. Wood (eds) *Play and Learning in the Early Years*. London: Sage, pp. 9–26.

Woods, A. (ed.) (2013) *Child-Initiated Play and Learning: Planning for Possibilities in the Early Years*. London: David Fulton.

Woods, A. (ed.) (2015) *The Characteristics of Effective Learning: Creating and Capturing the Possibilities in the Early Years*. London: David Fulton.

Woods, A. (ed.) (2016) *Examining Levels of Involvement in the Early Years: Engaging with Children's Possibilities*. London: David Fulton.

Index

adaption 7
Adventure Playground 110, 113, 118
affordance 63, 89, 96, 101, 109, 114, 119, 149
Appleton's habitat theory 74, 112
archaic consciousness 5, 62; experience 5
assimilation 7, 21, 22, 52, 134
Athey, C. 7, 94
attachment 8, 15, 20, 22–4, 37, 83, 85, 94, 109, 115, 119, 143
awe 48–9, 51, 55, 58–9, 64, 74, 98, 109

Bilton, H. 111, 113, 116, 124
biocultural 7, 144–5
biological predisposition 55; biologically programmed 63, 72
biophilia 43, 63, 103, 146; biophilic relationship 6
biophobia 103
Bird, L. & Drewery, W. 133–4
Bjorkland, D.F. & Pellegrini, A.D. 6, 18, 34, 112, 123, 146
Bodrova, E. & Leong, D.J. 135, 144, 146
Bowlby, J. 7
Boyd Cadwell, L. 126
Broadhead, P. 141
Broadhead, P. & Burt, A. 110, 111, 113, 128–9
Bronfenbrenner, U. 7, 18, 21, 34, 41, 48, 57, 66, 85, 108–9, 135, 148
bricolage 134
Brooker, L. 97, 99, 133, 135, 139, 146, 149

Bruce, T. 94, 135
Bruner, J. 7, 18, 22, 41, 84

Carr, M. 57, 96
Carson, R. 8, 49, 50–1, 66, 84
Casey, T. 111–13, 116, 119, 121, 124
Chawla, L. 36–7, 39, 49, 56, 62, 71, 74–5, 89, 109, 112, 119
Clark, A. 115
Cobb, E. 51, 56, 93, 114
communities of learners 147
continuous provision 124–5
Csíkszentmihályi, M. 63, 97, 121
Cuffaro, H.K. 99
cultural 4, 6, 12, 15–18, 21–4, 27–9, 115, 133, 135–6, 139, 141–2, 144–5, 147–150
Curtis, D. & Carter, M. 111, 113, 116, 124

Davey, A. 127, 143
Davis, J. & Elliott, S. 35–6, 43
Day, C. 116, 128
Derr, T. 119
Dewey, J. 4, 7, 56, 99, 101, 121, 135
disequilibrium 7, 134
Donaldson, M. 26, 41, 85, 141
Duckett, R. & Drummond, M.-J. 86
Dunn, A. & MacPhee, J. 110

Eaude, T. 49, 136
eco- 4, 41, 44–5, 55, 112
ecological 17, 33–4, 44, 48, 55–8, 66, 74, 85, 90, 101, 103, 114, 135, 140–1, 149

Index

ecological systems theory 18, 41, 84, 108–9, 148; ecological theory of human development 57
ecology 147
Edgington, M. 111, 113, 116
Elliott, S. 111, 113, 116–17
Engström, Y., Miettinen, R. & Punamaki, R.-L. 149
environmental 7–8, 19, 22, 24, 32, 34–8, 40, 43–5, 48, 52, 58, 63, 74, 98–9, 103, 108, 117, 119–20, 137, 144, 146
epigenesis 6
equilibrium 7
evolution 5, 33, 59, 64, 72, 74, 85, 98, 128; evolutionary 4–5, 17–18, 31, 35, 45, 74, 89, 112
experiential 8, 26, 28, 44, 100, 107, 135
experiential education 99–100

Faarlund, N. 5, 147
Fjortoft, I. 86
forest school 16, 22, 38, 40, 44–5, 51–4, 73–4, 80, 88
friluftsliv 55, 87
Froebel, F. 56, 108, 121, 123, 134–5

Gaia hypothesis 57, 65
Gardner, H. 7, 32, 121
Garrick, R. 111, 113, 116, 124
Gaunt, C. 44–5
Gibson, E.J. 74, 96, 112, 114
Gilligan, D. 87
Goleman, D. 121
Gray, P. 35, 145
Greenman, J. 112–13, 118, 126, 147
Griffiths, J. 35
guided participation 16, 21, 58, 109, 148
Gussin-Paley, V. 52

habitat theory 74, 112
Hakkarainen, P. 87, 141
Hall, K., Murphy, P. & Soler, J. 21
Hay, D. & Nye, R. 49, 50, 53, 55, 85, 113, 144
Heerwagen, J.H. & Orians, G.H. 33, 146
heft 35
Heft, H. & Chawla, L. 112, 119

heuristic 63, 144
Hocking, M. 117
holistic 1, 5, 57, 71, 90, 118, 143
Holt, J. 95, 142
Hughes, B. 141, 145–6
human evolution 59, 72
hunter gathering 85

imagination 43, 50, 52, 62–3, 66, 75, 78, 80, 84, 86, 90, 97, 99, 100, 107, 109, 110, 118, 119, 127, 136–7, 140, 144
instinct 6, 27, 35, 63, 78, 87–8, 98, 109, 145, 147, 149
Isaacs, S. 12, 56, 108, 135

Jarvis, P. 144
joint attention 16, 40, 74

Kaarby, K.M.E. 137, 142
Kahn Jr., P.H. & Kellert, S.R. 5, 8, 13, 15, 45, 108, 116
Katz, L.G. 97, 103
Keown, D. 65
Kimes Myers, B. 48–9, 52–3, 56–8
Knight, S. 80, 111, 116, 120
Kyttä, M. 114

Laevers, F. 63, 68, 97, 100
landscape 7, 35, 37, 40–1, 43, 49, 55, 74–5, 80, 87–9, 110, 112, 114–15, 117, 124–5, 138, 148–9
Leuven scales 68
levels of involvement 63, 68, 100, 125, 127, 138, 143
Lindqvist, G. 87
Little Muddy Boots 19–20, 22, 36, 54, 67–8, 98
loose parts 43, 84, 86, 114; loose parts theory 43, 64, 84; *see also* Nicholson, S.
Louv, R. 49, 56, 58, 85, 89, 108

MacNaughton, G. 6, 85, 134
magic 5, 19, 59, 66, 74, 78–80, 82, 83, 84, 86, 89, 90, 109, 119
Malaguzzi, L. 26, 42, 67, 96
Marfo, K. & Biersteker, L. 147
Maxwell. L.E., Mitchell, M.R. & Evans, G.W. 111, 113, 116

May, P., Ashford, E. & Bottle, G. 18, 22, 68, 126
Maynard, T. & Waters, J. 12
McEwan, V. 24
McMillan, M. 56, 108, 124
Meade, A. 57
mediation 15, 18, 26
Metzner, R. 49, 56, 65–6
Michael, P. 103
Mills, J. 5, 9, 12, 14, 18, 51, 79, 80
mindfulness 50
Ministry of Education 3, 4, 15
Montessori, M. 84, 108, 112, 121, 135
Moore, R.C. & Cosco, N.G. 38, 44, 57, 65
Moore, R. & Young, D. 40, 43–4, 114, 128, 148
Moran, M. & Brown, V. 84, 139
mosaic approach 115
Moyles, J. 135, 140, 144
mud kitchen 20, 68, 123, 125, 128
mystery 54–5, 58, 74, 79–80, 86, 122, 141, 149
mystic experiences 49, 64, 79

Nabhan, G.P. & St. Antoine, S. 43
Nicholson, S. 109–11; *see also* loose parts
Nutbrown, C. 94

Ouvrey, M. 41
Owens, R. 56

participatory appropriation 21
Pestalozzi, J. 56, 108, 121
Piaget, J. 7, 32, 41, 83, 94, 112, 121, 140
Playworlds 87
projects 2, 7, 32, 53, 68, 87, 104, 109–10

reciprocal 15–16, 31, 44, 48, 57–8, 82
Reedy, T. 57
Reggio 2, 7, 26, 44, 66, 89, 96, 108, 126
religious 49, 55–6, 59, 80
rhizome 6, 66
Rivkin, M.S. 35–6, 111, 118
Robinson, E. 49, 52, 103
Robson, S. 100
Rogoff, B. 18, 20–3, 26, 28–9, 147
Roszak, T. 48–9, 55–6, 90–1

Rousseau, J.-J. 56, 121
Rupp, R. 5, 70–1, 73, 75, 80
Ryder, D. vii, 2, 18, 20, 25–6, 34, 37, 62, 64, 66, 85, 93

Santer, J., Griffiths, C. & Goodall, D. 135, 137, 140–1, 145
schema 33, 69, 93–4, 138; schematic 93–4, 136, 143
Scott, D. 59, 86
Smidt, S. 135
socialisation 42, 115
socio-constructivist 24, 135, 138, 141
socio-cultural 4, 12, 15–16, 27–8, 48–9, 108, 148
socio-emotional development 135
spiritual 5–8, 17, 44, 48–9, 50, 52–3, 55, 57–9, 63, 73, 82–3, 85–6, 90, 109, 117, 139, 141
Steiner, R. 55–6, 71, 87, 96, 108
sustained shared thinking 26, 135

Taonga Maori 4
Taylor, A. 55–6, 58, 135, 145–6
Taylor-Coleridge, S. 55
Te Whāriki 108
Thoreau, H.D. 56, 87–8
Thornton, L. & Brunton, P. 26
Titman, W. 36, 41, 115
Tordsson, B. 55, 88–9
Tovey, H. 84, 111, 116, 119, 124, 141
transcend 117
Tuan, Y.-F. 23, 28, 37, 42, 44–6, 58, 83

Utz, G. 66

van Oers, B. 99, 148
Vasta, R. 1, 18, 21, 27, 34, 98, 133, 139
Vecchi, V. & Giudici, C. 73
Vygotsky, L. 7, 25, 28, 84, 121, 136, 144–6

Waite, S., Huggins, H. & Wickett, K. 142
Waller, T. 86
Waller, T., Whitmarsh, J. & Clarke, J. 98
Warden, C. 73
Wardle, L. & Vesty, S. 53
Wattchow, B. 89

Index

Wattchow, B. & Brown, M. 5, 36, 45, 115
Watts, A. 110, 113, 116, 124
Webster, S. 52
well-being 7–8, 12, 24, 53, 55–7, 63
White, J. 63, 70, 72, 88, 118
White, J. & Woolley, H. 74, 112, 118–9, 142
White, R. & Stoeklin, V. 63, 87, 103
Williams-Siegfredsen, J. 111, 113, 116, 121
Wilson, R. 140
Wilson, R.A. 51
Winnicott, D. 23, 136
wonder 12, 25, 48, 50–1, 58–9, 63, 74, 95
Woods, A. 19, 93, 100, 101, 125, 127, 137, 139, 143
Wordsworth, W. 55–6

zone of proximal development 59, 84, 100